MARKETING
YOUR
BUSINESS

The Daily Telegraph
ESSENTIAL MANAGEMENT TECHNIQUES

MARKETING YOUR BUSINESS

JEREMY BOND & MIKE TINTNER
THE MOORGATE GROUP PLC

Published by Telegraph Publications,
Peterborough Court, At South Quay,
181 Marsh Wall, London E14 9SR

Whilst every care has been taken to ensure the accuracy of the contents of this
work, no responsibility for loss occasioned to any person acting or refraining
from action as a result of any statement in it can be accepted.

Series Editor: Marlene Garsia

Typeset by Bookworm Typesetters, Manchester
Printed in Great Britain by Biddles Ltd, Guildford

British Library Cataloguing in Publication Data
Bond, Jeremy
    Marketing your business.———(Essential
    management techniques).
    1. Marketing
    I. Title II. Tintner, Mike III. Series
    658.8   HF5415

ISBN 0–86367–225–6

Contents

Introduction

What is marketing?

The answer to this question has come in many forms over the years with some practitioners even cloaking the process in mystery, using terms such as 'geodemographic marketing segments', 'environmental scanning', 'marketing mixes'. They pour out the jargon with the newcomer being left enormously confused about what marketing really involves. But marketing is basically a commonsense process which anyone can understand and master.

The first step is to understand that companies need to market their products because we live in a large and complex world. In a small village, producers and consumers know each other. The local baker does not need to advertise his wares because everyone is familiar with what he sells. But with national or international markets producers and consumers are so far apart that they are unknown to each other. Consequently, finding out who your consumers are, where they live, and what they think about your product can be a major task especially if you are dealing with thousands of customers. Hence the need to market your product(s).

The second step in understanding marketing is to realise that it is much broader than most people imagine. It is not just selling, for example, or advertising (two of the commonest assumptions), but identifying the consumers of a product, fitting the product to their needs, and then selling them the product at a price that will yield a profit. Advertising and selling are only parts of this process.

Historically, marketing has been defined as the 'four Ps' – product, promotion, place and price – which involve developing a product, promoting it to the consumers, deciding the place to sell it, and setting the price. Each part of the process is important, although in practice, of course, some parts – promotion particularly – will get more emphasis.

Modern marketing theorists stress that marketing should be principally about satisfying consumer needs, which means first being prepared to change the product. The theorists are faithful to the spirit of Adam Smith who wrote that:

Consumption is the sole end and purpose of all production; and the interest of the producer ought to be attended to, only so far as it may be necessary for promoting that of the consumer.

In practice, a company will have certain capabilities and may not be able to change that easily. If a chocolate manufacturer such as Cadbury finds customers prefer a 'more squishy' chocolate bar, it may be able to create one rapidly. Other companies are more constrained. If a carmaker were to find that what people really want is not so much a car as a cross between a car and helicopter, it might not have the expertise to develop such a machine. Every company has its limitations. Actual marketing may be more about selling the products you already have than some theorists might like to admit. Nevertheless, the ideal of fitting product precisely to customer needs should never be abandoned.

Satisfying consumer needs means, in the second instance, that when promoting a product you have to look at it from the consumer's viewpoint rather than your own. In practice, that is neither as easy nor as obvious as it sounds. If you have spent a great deal of time and energy creating, producing and distributing a product, you are naturally full of your labours and eager to communicate them to the world. You want to proclaim exactly how many ball bearings your new widget contains and how long it took to make. But such information is often totally irrelevant to the consumer. All he may want to know from your advertising and literature is what your product does, and what it can do for him. Will your widget, for example, kill all known garden flies?

Tell him anything more and you may irritate, bore and even obscure your main message. So 'satisfy consumer needs' is a very meaningful injunction and one, unfortunately, still neglected by many marketing people.

Marketing disciplines

There are various disciplines involved in marketing, each of which may entail a separate department in a large organisation. The major disciplines are set out in the following illustration.

Table 1 Marketing disciplines

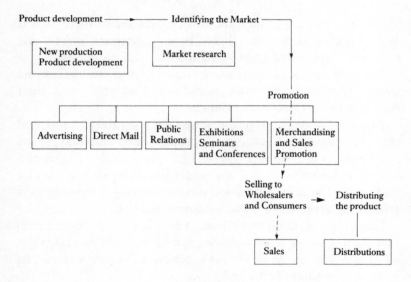

We shall be considering most of these disciplines in the course of this book.

In a large organisation the marketing manager should be familiar with all of them, able to interact and communicate with the different specialists in each section, enabling him to design and control a company's overall marketing policy. (The marketing manager normally controls policy for various brands, the brand manager for just one.)

Directors of small businesses may have to handle their entire marketing singlehanded. Ideally, though, they too should know something about all the different disciplines, otherwise they are likely to miss many opportunities. It is important, for example, to realise that advertising may not be the only way to promote a company. Public relations (PR) and direct mail may be even more effective. Although marketing may be commonsense, it is still easy to overlook the obvious approach.

Outline of the book

We will be looking at the process of marketing in three stages. We are not suggesting that this is the only approach, merely that it is useful, and is practised by many successful companies.

Part I of this book is on analysis: identifying the market; the needs of consumers, both actual and potential; and their reactions to the company's product.

Part 2 on strategy. Having analysed the potential for increased sales, and any need to change the product, the marketing person must now form a *marketing plan*. That will set sales targets and outline a marketing mix – a product development plan, and a budget for the different means of promotion – which can best achieve the targets and reach the largest market.

Part 3 is on implementation. The plan must be put into execution. One or more agencies must be chosen to design the advertising, write the direct mail, organise the publicity and so forth, and be properly briefed.

It must be stressed that the whole process is an open-ended cycle, the stages are not isolated from each other. The marketing manager should always, in principle, be able to go back or forward a stage. An excellent advertising idea might dictate a change in packaging. A brilliant PR programme might call for a different media mix, diverting more money to the latter and less to advertising. Similarly, planning marketing involves thinking forward to implementation, to what kind of promotion, for example, could be achieved with a given budget.

It is hardly surprising that we talk about marketing 'campaigns'. Successful marketing – marketing for results – does involve very careful planning, with as much thought and attention to detail as a sophisticated military campaign.

Case History No 1. Marketing mix: Cadbury's Wispa

The launch of Cadbury's Wispa chocolate bar is a classic example of a highly successful marketing campaign involving many different marketing disciplines.

This product began as a response to consumer wants. Cadbury's market research revealed that there was a growing demand for lighter confectionery as Rowntree's bubbly Aero chocolate bar was competing hotly with its own Dairy Milk bar. And Cadbury's product development team took five years to perfect a pure chocolate alternative, the new Wispa bar. This was test launched in the Tyne Tees area, an area which has about 5 per cent of total UK spending power. Demand was so great that supplies ran out after eight weeks. Cadbury's subsequently took the product off the market and built a new larger factory costing £11 million so as to increase production.

Cadbury's then started a major television advertising campaign (through Young and Rubicam) and a PR programme (through Leslie Bishop) to portray the bar as a new kind of eating experience, with a 'Bite it and believe it' theme, spending £7 million.

Wispa was relaunched in the Tyne Tees area in October 1983, with parachutists dropping in the first supplies, a fireworks party being held, and Wispa bars being handed out in hospitals and schools. Later there was a promotional offer, 'Wispa mania', featuring mugs, pens and other goods stamped with the Wispa name, plus an offer of five free bars in return for 25 wrappers. Over the first three years there were one and a half million consumer applications for Wispa offers, an amazing level of interest.

Part I: Analysis

It is very tempting, when confronted with the problem of marketing a company and its products, to charge in with immediate solutions.

Well, if I were selling that range of trousers, I'd change the advertising, smarten up their image, link them perhaps with some modern rock band, make them generally much more attractive to younger people.

Clearly, we are not always overawed by the marketing process, often fancying ourselves as instant experts. But no matter what our marketing qualifications, or status, it will help us to stand back at first and analyse the overall situation of a company.

- What are the company's goals?
- What are the products it is selling?
- Who is it trying to sell to, and what are their needs?

These questions, particularly the first two, may seem very irritating and so basic as to be obvious. Yet, properly pursued, they can lead to answers which are often unexpected and nearly always fruitful.

1
Defining the Company's Goals

One of the very first things a marketing manager should do when defining a company's marketing problems, is to ask: 'What are the company's goals?' Broadly speaking, a company can have one of four orientations. It can be:

- Production-orientated.
- Technology-orientated.
- Sales-orientated.
- Marketing-orientated.

In a production-orientated company, most of the energy goes into improving the efficiency and quality of production and bringing down product cost. The product is then handed over to the sales force almost as an afterthought. It is supposed to be so good that they cannot help but sell it.

The classic example was the Ford motor company in the early days of Model T cars, which paid most attention to the production line, with Henry Ford insisting that customers could have any colour car they wanted as long as it was black.

The production-led company may fare well as long as the product it produces really is measurably superior to or cheaper than its rivals. But the danger is losing touch with the market. Customer demand and the competition soon forced Ford to change.

The technology-oriented company is driven by innovation. It looks at existing product technology and sets out to make improvements which it feels customers ought to want, often without consulting them.

There are many product technologies which tempt producers

in this way. Anyone who knows about computers, for example, knows that there are all kinds of ways they can be improved – they can be made faster, more integrated in functions, given better graphics, and so on. Consequently there is a natural urge for makers to concentrate on producing the next generation of computer with these exciting new features.

There are dangers here too. Customers may not want the new technology for a whole variety of reasons. Polaroid, which is generally recognized as a technology-led company as distinct from the marketing or consumer-led Kodak, introduced a new and far superior camera in the 1970s, the SX-70, and at a far higher price. They found out the hard way that consumers were not prepared to pay the extra money.

Conversely, Amstrad showed what could be done with a highly technological product such as the personal computer, when it marketed the PCW812 not as a piece of technology, with so much storage, so much speed, and other features, but simply to satisfy a basic consumer need in providing a replacement for the typewriter. Here was a truly user-friendly concept that the ordinary, techno-illiterate consumer could understand; the machine was a roaring success, selling in the hundreds of thousands.

It may not be possible to gauge market reactions so accurately with many new products. While a totally new product, such as a voice-driven typewriter, may be something that people obviously need, they might not know they need it, or not know how to use it. Any opinions that they therefore voice to market researchers may be very misleading, and the marketing manager may have to go on his 'gut feeling' instead of their replies.

In a sales-orientated company, the emphasis is on building up volume sales. The higher the sales figures, so they reason, the better the company and the people in it; bigger, better, best – a simple equation.

However, increasing sales can sometimes lead to dis-economies of scale. If salesmen are pushed to increase volume, they may spend more and more time chasing smaller and smaller customers, pushing up costs, with the end result that volume goes up and profits go down. Increased sales are, as a rule, only desirable as long as they produce increased profits. The marketing-orientated company is the ideal. Here the goal must be to find out and keep in mind the needs of customers, and balance those needs against company capabilities in order to make the maximum profit rather than sales. Lower sales concentrated on a few, high-paying, volume-buying customers may be much more profitable in the long run.

The ideal of the marketing-orientated company may often be impossible to achieve. The one-product, up-and-coming company may not be capable of the same sophisticated marketing as a mature company with various ranges of products, and capabilities in many fields. It will not have the same budget for promotion, the same resources for researching the market, the same capability for responding to consumer's needs. Marketing managers should therefore have a sense of their company's immediate limitations as well as ultimate potential.

Another question worth asking at the very beginning, when preparing a marketing strategy, is the one posed by Theodore C Levitt in a famous *Harvard Business Review* article: *What business are we in?* The more loosely, or to put it another way, the more comprehensively that question is answered, the greater the possible scope of a company.

What business, for example, is IBM in? Is it just in the business of providing computer hardware and software? That would be an obvious conclusion, and a limiting one. IBM sees itself as being in the business of 'problem-solving'. Similarly, a forward-thinking managing director such as Peter Carr of Queensway, which sells mainly furniture and floor coverings, sees his business as 'selling *rooms*, not just furniture'. And, increasingly, a whole variety of financial institutions, such as banks, building societies and insurance groups, are diversifying and redefining their business as selling 'personal financial services' rather than merely traditional banking services, or mortgages, or insurance. (A recent television commercial for the Midland Bank, which markets itself as 'the listening bank', was a perfect embodiment of the marketing ideal, showing a customer coming into a bank and dictating to initially surprised managers the precise kind of bank account he would like – the Vector.)

The broader the definition of a company's goals, the greater the stimulus to provide new products and services, and extend and improve old ones. IBM's product range only caters for so many kinds of 'problem-solving'. There are therefore all kinds of gaps that IBM could be filling. Similarly, Peter Carr's 'room concept' has led him to ask why Queensway should be selling customers beds and sofas and then sending them elsewhere for bedding, curtains and mirrors. Why not fill those gaps too? The broad-ranging approach to defining company goals can extend the horizons of everyone from the one-product, one-service company to the giant corporation.

2
Defining the Product

Product lifecycle

Once the marketing manager has considered the company's overall situation he can now examine individual products in detail.

The immediate question to ask of any product which will inevitably determine the marketing effort is: What stage has it reached in its lifecycle? Every product has a lifecycle, being born at one point and dying at another. An awareness of a product's mortality is a prerequisite for effective marketing.

Some brands, such as Coca-Cola and Kellogg's Cornflakes, may seem to be impregnable, but for every famous brand that has survived there are scores more that have not. For every Pedigree Chum there is a Kennomeat, for every Dulux a Berger paints, and for every Heineken a Double Diamond.

In some sectors, product turnover can be terrifying. A recent survey of the grocery sector revealed that as many as 24 per cent of products were not merchandised the following year.

The theory of the product lifecycle holds that every product passes through four stages.

Stage 1 Introduction. The first stage is the introduction of the product into the marketplace. An enormous initial investment often has to be made in creating stocks, launch advertising and promotions, with more special efforts made by salesmen and management. Profits are likely to be minimal.

Stage 2 Growth. In the next stage, sales grow rapidly. If this is a new kind of product, there may be little competition. Profits are likely to be greatest.

Stage 3 Maturity. Now the product is likely to face increased competition. Prices may have to be lowered, advertising increased, and costs may rise. Even if sales continue to rise the profitability might fall.

Stage 4 Saturation. Yet more competitors enter the market. The supply of competitive products outstrips demand. Prices have to be cut still further and this time sales decline as well as profits. Finally, the product has to be withdrawn.

Increased competition is not the only reason why a product may die. It can become technologically outmoded – the electro-mechanical cash register cedes to the purely electronic version, the Swiss analog watch gives way to the Japanese quartz watch. Although the product lifecycle theory is only a theory it can prove extremely useful in planning a marketing campaign.

If the marketing manager considers that the product is in Stage 4, marketing should probably be abandoned. On the other hand, the product may just need an extra push to revitalise it. Putting theories into practice is never that straightforward.

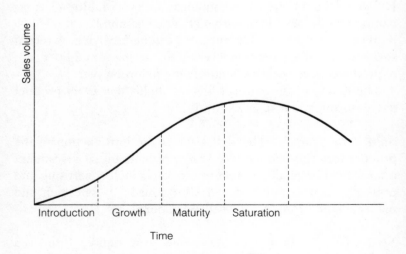

Figure 1   Product life cycle

Product positioning

When considering which stage a product has reached, the marketing manager must review its positioning. Positioning is the particular attribute of a product that is emphasised by marketing and most immediately acknowledged or recognised by the consumer – the attribute that makes a product stand out from its competitors.

The question to ask yourself is whether your product is positioned correctly or, in the case of a new product, how it should be positioned. There are almost as many possible attributes to stress as there are products to market, although there are a few tried and tested ones which keep recurring.

The most immediate type of attribute is market share. Is your product a market leader? 'We are Number 1' is an oft-repeated claim, and almost irresistible if you can make it. Number 2 is not so bad, either. Avis achieved great things with its 'We are Number 2, so we try harder' campaign. Sanka in the USA even sells itself as the 'third largest-selling brand of coffee in the USA'!

Then there is the quality of the product. It may be the fastest, largest, most powerful – a quality for which consumers may be prepared to pay more. Consider too the price. You could be the cheapest, (or the most expensive) on the market. You may have more features than any competitor.

Whatever the positioning of a product, the ideal is to go for some unique feature or Unique Selling Proposition (USP), which no competitive product can claim and which is important to the consumer. Never go for more than two features because no matter how many separate features or facilities a product may boast, consumers, bombarded as they are day and night by one sales story after another – will only be able to retain one or two features.

Sometimes a repositioning of the product will be called for, perhaps because the market is changing, or, most significantly, because sales are changing.

Another potential problem is that a product may have been positioned too cheaply. MFI, one of the largest furniture retailers in the UK and also one of the largest advertisers, has recently been trying to upgrade its discount furniture image to move away from the 'warehouse' concept which inspired its great success of the 1970s. MFI found that customers were developing increasingly sophisticated tastes in the style of merchandise and the shopping environment they required, so it redesigned its stores, introducing a new colour scheme and layout.

By contrast, Ratners has radically changed the jewellery business in Britain by making jewellery cheaper, not more expensive. Gerald Ratner, the firm's dynamic chief executive, inspired by retailers such as Dixons and Marks and Spencer, sacrilegiously cut prices by as much as a half, and filled his shop windows with posters promoting the goods inside. The result was a major expansion of the market, bringing in, among others, teenagers who would never have thought of buying jewellery before it was brought into their price range. In two years, profits increased nearly fourfold.

A common, basic type of repositioning is to 'modernise' a product. As products grow older, so they come to seem outdated, and very skilful repositioning may be needed. A classic example is Ovaltine which had become 'almost a byword for old fashioned' according to marketing manager Russell Willey. Ovaltine is still perceived in Britain as a 'food drink' for night-time consumption, but the market for such drinks is steadily declining. So a major repositioning was undertaken, depicting Ovaltine in television commercials as a drink that could be taken anytime, anywhere – and helping to bring about a gradual recovery in sales.

A similar and even more effective exercise was undertaken recently for Beecham Foods' Lucozade. The original drink was first invented as long ago as 1927. During the 1950s, 1960s and 1970s Lucozade was promoted as a drink particularly suitable for periods of convalescence, with its advertising primarily targeted at housewives. In the 1980s Beecham decided that they could move away from this 'convalescence' platform to enter the major volume, soft drink market.

The first step was to introduce a quarter-litre bottle. This helped extend the Lucozade drinking environment beyond the home with a series of commercials showing how Lucozade's glucose base could help even healthy people get through the day more easily.

The real revolution, though, came in 1983, when Beecham Foods departed completely from its traditional stance, now targeting a new audience of men and children. Advertisements featured Olympic decathlete Daley Thompson using the product in order to give the campaign more impact and propel the drink into the modern world. Next, when research showed that the container that teenagers preferred was the 330ml can, Lucozade began producing it in 1985. Again, Daley Thompson was used in a 20-second commercial showing him sprinting down the track, and afterwards refreshing himself with a can of Lucozade.

The sales figures for 1986 – the can had only been launched in July 1985 – show that Lucozade smashed all sales records that year with £33 million of Lucozade being sold in Britain in 1984; in 1986 the figure leapt to £52 million. But the success did not stop there. Beecham Foods have gone on to introduce a range of barley-flavoured Lucozade drinks.

More recently there was a more homely but equally exciting example of repositioning in the advertising treatment of Torbay. Torquay, Brixham and Paignton are not immediately the most exciting or exotic of holiday resorts. Tim Whitehead, tourism officer of the Torbay Tourism Office and a marketing man by profession, had a very unexciting £150,000 budget with which to market them. In 1983 he decided to let Travis Dale, an offshoot of the major advertising agency Collett Dickinson Pearce, handle his account and gave them a heady £100,000 to play with. It was a very difficult situation for many reasons, including the fact that fewer and fewer holidaymakers were coming to Torbay – there had been a 22 per cent drop in tourist nights between 1977 and 1984 – while tourism remained vital to the region, providing some 30 per cent of local employment.

Travis Dale came up with a brilliant solution. It devised a series of posters repositioning the area as 'The English Riviera'. It was a solution in every sense. The decline in tourist numbers was arrested and in fact they are now growing again in a way very similar to Torbay's bumper 1977 season.

It is hardly surprising that 'positioning' is such a buzzword in modern marketing, for this can be the vital ingredient in making a product succeed.

Branding

It is just as easy to confuse a brand with a product name, as it is to confuse marketing with selling. In fact, a brand is much more than a distinctive name, it is the entire personality of a product, as comprised by packaging, positioning, advertising, and the consumers' general associations with the product.

Branding can be essential in a market crowded with competitors all making similar claims for their own products. Without it a product can be merely a commodity, bought only out of necessity, whose price is at the whim of supply and demand.

Branding is most commonly used in the market of packaged or Fast Moving Consumer Goods (FMCG) such as toothpaste, cigarettes, beer, breakfast cereals or light bulbs. The intrinsic differences between competing products can be relatively small – can you really tell the difference between Coca-Cola and Pepsi Cola? Branding can make the difference.

There are some, of course, who would fiercely contest this point of view. They would argue that traditional branding is finished in the UK. Nowadays it is retailers with their own brands – especially stores such as Sainsbury, Marks and Spencer and Tesco – which are increasingly in control, while manufacturers of named brands are either dying or licking their wounds. Many consumers perceive own brands to be of equal quality to those of leading manufacturers if not better.

But named brands are by no means dead. What has happened is that the larger ones have survived while only the smaller ones, the number three and four brands, have gone to the wall, thanks in part to the big stores' policy of stocking at least one big brand side by side with their own-label.

The investment in marketing FMCG products and creating

'brand awareness' can often be formidable. In some cases it will account for up to 40 per cent of the retail price of the product. The cost of launching new brands is particularly formidable. The eight weeks' television exposure that some managers might think essential for a new brand could easily cost a million pounds. That is a huge amount for many manufacturers. The sum of £10m for a retailer represents only a tiny percentage of his total sales, but for an average manufacturer it could equal 5 per cent of his sales and the whole of his net profits. Meanwhile, media costs are spiralling upwards, well ahead of inflation, further increasing the pressures on manufacturers. Interestingly, many have responded by doggedly maintaining that the money spent on advertising protects their identities.

Bear in mind too that brands are built slowly. Graeme Christie, new brand development manager at IDV, calculates that it took 10 years to establish the very successful Bailey's Irish Cream. Yet 'Malibu broke all the rules and took 6 years'.

The market depends on its manufacturers. The immediate reason is that they are much better able to innovate. They usually have much more intellectual fire-power. With food, for example, there is only one major own-brand company that keeps innovating (and keeps being copied), and it is not hard to think who it is – Marks and Spencer.

The name is certainly a crucial part of branding. It must express the personality of the product accurately and distinctively, so enormous care should be taken in choosing a name. KP Choc Dips is a case in point.

This was KP's first venture into a new field. It was marketing what had originally been a Japanese product called Yan Yan. That name hardly reflected the product's nature to British ears, so KP considered a variety of alternatives including: Nibble Stix, Joy Stix, Choc Stix, Big Dipper, Soldiers, and Pooh Stix.

But research revealed that these all had wrong connotations. Some were childish, some too flashy and American, some positively rude. The problem was handed over to Holmes and Marchant Graphics which came up with the straight descriptive Choc Dips. It was a story with a very happy ending. Within 5 months, 10 million units had been sold, making KP Choc Dips the most successful launch in United Biscuits' history.

There are many agencies which specialise in developing new names, among them KAE Development, Novamark, and Brand New Product Origination, a wholly-owned subsidiary of the Michael Peters Group. This may seem surprising at first. Could advertising agencies not produce names by themselves? They could and do. But when you think that major industrial empires are founded on strange, exotic, and powerful names such as Kodak, Durex and Coca-Cola, perhaps the existence of name specialists is not so surprising after all.

They often use very different techniques. KAE Development has regular creative brainstorming sessions which involve every level of management and staff. An associate director will manage such sessions, spurring participants on to think freely of ever more bizarre names and associations – what could be more bizarre than Durex? – and then checking ideas with questions like: 'Will you feel entirely comfortable asking for a can of 'Pussy Fresh'?' (a suggested name for a new cat food).

Some specialists have distinguished themselves. An agency such as Novamark can boast a string of famous invented names, including Metro, Montego, Maestro, Kestrel and Homebase. Its method is significantly different. It invites a completely freelance panel of participants, who are recruited through small advertisements in *The Times* and *Private Eye*. The qualities demanded, for example, include an addiction to crossword puzzles. The people finally selected range from cartoonists, salespersons and housewives, to systems analysts and solicitors. Sessions are very much unstructured. The emphasis will be on pouring out as many names as possible and, after a two-hour session, they may have as many as 2,000.

Product names can often be very useful in articulating a product's nature, rather than merely evoking it. A major example was the Rainbow Group of Financial products, developed for Eagle Star Insurance. Eagle Star was branching out from insurance into investment, introducing a whole new range of investment products from investment bonds to unit trusts, and it needed a name. Rainbow was brilliant both as a new name and a new concept. The idea involved all these financial products being colour-coded according to the degree of risk (and investment opportunity) involved. It was such a simple idea, perfectly crystallised in the umbrella Rainbow concept, and it made investing, which had until then so baffled so many, a simple process accessible to everyone. The Rainbow products were a major success.

There are many other criteria that a name must satisfy, besides reflecting the product's nature. It must be legally registered as a trademark – there is no point in producing a name that already exists in the market place, because that will not only lead to legal wrangling, it will also confuse consumers. Also, the name must be easy to pronounce.

It is not unusual for brand names to be developed under an umbrella brand image such as Rainbow. Lending the brand image to a number of products in this way has to be thought through in detail if the extension is not to backfire. In all cases, the subsidiary products must relate credibly to consumers' associations with the master brand image. It is almost as inconceivable that the Rover Group should start marketing a range of washing powders as that IBM should launch a chain of florist shops.

Packaging

Packaging, as with the brand name, must harmonise with the nature of the product. It is like the candelabra sitting on Liberace's piano. And it is the last opportunity the product has of 'talking' to the consumer before purchase, especially if it is resting on shop or supermarket shelves.

That said, packaging is more relevant to some goods than others, particularly the FMCG's. Consumer durables, such as cars, have to rest on the overall excellence of their design and the nature and reputation of their marque.

Where packaging is important, every feature must be analysed in depth. The logo, the graphics, the colours and the packaging materials must proclaim what kind of experience the consumer can expect, and what kind of consumer the producer is trying to reach – for example, the young and progressive or the older and more conservative, male or female.

Different colours have different connotations. Red, for example, implies excitement, green safety, black should be used with care outside fashion items, and blue and white are fairly recessive.

Case History No 2. Packaging: Appletise

The introduction of Appletise is a fascinating example of the kind of detailed thinking that should go into packaging. Originally, before being packaged in its present form, Appletise was just another drink brought to England by South African Breweries. New product development company Craton Lodge Knight (CLK) looked at it and realised that here was the Holy Grail of the soft drinks industry – an adult soft drink, something that everyone had been looking for. But how to package it correctly?

The packaging could not be child-oriented, as with Cydrax and Peardrax, and it had to appeal to both men and women. CLK came up with a small, hard, masculine bottle shape. The smallness of the bottle designated this as a special drink. The hard contours gave it unisex appeal, because whereas men tend to be put off by feminine shapes, women are not put off by the reverse.

Then the product was launched in careful sequence. First as a bottle in pubs, and as a multipack in supermarkets. That way women started ordering it in pubs and then bought it in supermarkets to take home. Husbands tried it at home and, liking it, started ordering it in pubs. Then and only then, once early usership had established this in consumers' minds as a special drink, was a big bottle version launched. Had the big bottle been launched too early it would have had negative connotations with Appleade-type products. Compare the lack of success of competitive product Kiri.

Appletise achieved quite outstanding results. It was launched in 1983 and in 1984 was awarded the accolade of Number 1 new product by the licensed trade. Only two years later, in 1986, it had built a 56 per cent share of the sparkling pure apple juice market, a market it was largely responsible for creating, and had established itself as one of the adult soft drink successes.

Apparently simple packaging was an essential element in Appletise establishing and completely dominating a new market. 'The fact that you can't see any of that strategy is a measure of our achievement,' explained Don Knight, chairman of CLK.

There are also more mundane considerations to packaging, over and above how it defines a product. Packaging must be safe and convenient. It is no good packaging an attractive breakfast cereal into a box that will not fit neatly on a supermarket shelf, or into the shopper's trolley. Packaging should be durable. It should not be easily damaged in the distribution chain, so that it becomes shabby and undesirable by the time it reaches the shelves. Packaging can supply valuable information on products and how they are selling to retailers. Computerisation means that stores can now work out exactly how much profit they make on each different product in the store, and even compare the difference made to sales by two separate types of packaging.

There may also be complex legal regulations to master governing the safety of the container, as is the case, for example, with household products such as bleach. Many products, such as pharmaceuticals and cigarettes, have to make space on their packaging for mandatory government warnings. Cellophane wrappings and aerosols can be dangerous if abused, and must say so. Processed food has to carry product information on its packaging. With other products there are ecological considerations. Friends of the Earth, for example, have long protested against the use of CFCs (chlorofluorocarbons) in aerosols, claiming that they deplete the earth's ozone layer. Since about one-third of the 697 million aerosols in this country use CFC as a propellant, this could become a matter of practical, if not moral concern for many marketers and manufacturers should FOE and other conservationists effectively get their message across.

If the product has been on sale for some time it is always worth thinking about revamping the packaging. But the changes may have to be very subtle. Changing the HP Sauce bottle, for example, was very difficult. The problem was that the bottle seemed rather jaded and too 1950s for the tastes of younger consumers. Yet many features of the bottle were clearly sacrosanct, such as the logo, the Houses of Parliament picture, and the basic shape. Conran Associates were given the job, and ended up chamfering the edges and recessing the label, among other changes, with the end result that the bottle is now strongly preferred by younger consumers, although appealing marginally less to existing users. It was a price the producers considered well worth paying.

A still more impressive revamp was undertaken on Twiglets. The product group manager at Nabisco had realised that Twiglets was being severely undersold. He saw that Twiglets needed to be repositioned and that packaging would be a major pack of that task. In fact, the positioning of the product had not been changed in over 50 years. Twiglets had always been bought for the special occasion, and had been largely ignored by the snacks market, the market where most of the growth was coming. And yet Twiglets would be ideal, Bishop believed, for this larger market.

The route he took was to reposition the brand as a snack suitable for eating on any occasion. He also decided to emphasise the healthy nature of Twiglets. The first crucial packaging action taken was to replace the old traditional box with new, more attractive foil bags. These keep the product much fresher. The design of the new pack was given to Michael Peters, who emerged from a long process of research with something very distinctive. The new pack sets sharp primary colours against a white background, and uses pictures of celery and tomato to give the product a crisp, fresh feel and suitable healthy associations. The branding was given a much more powerful emphasis by the addition of a blue keyline around the lettering.

The results have been staggering. Sales rose by some 90 per cent. In addition, the new packaging enabled Bishop to extend distribution to cover the biscuit, snacks and pub markets. Bishop is, not surprisingly, a firm believer in the power of design.

Own-brand labels are also coming in for more design

attention. Tesco, for example, has dedicated itself to relaunching and repackaging all of its own-label lines as part of its general policy of changing its image from an economy store, to one that can compete with the other big names.

Asda is also upgrading some of its images. Mary Lewis, director at Lewis Moberly (who did much of the wines and spirits packaging design for Tesco), has produced a series of labels for Asda wines which combine classic typography with stylish modern illustrations. According to *Marketing* magazine, these are 'good enough to steam off the bottle and frame on the wall'. The branding is very discreet, for Asda's name is only printed in tiny letters at the bottom.

The tendency in the past has been very much to produce discreet own brand designs. People usually stick to, and know their way around a particular store, so their attention does not have to be seized by screaming colours. In addition, an own brand can be designed to fit into the exact location that a store wants, creating, if so desired, an attractive uniform block of colour.

Another important branch not so much of packaging as of general design – but still worth considering – is that of corporate identity. This has been a frequent subject of conversation among marketing people because of the controversy about the new Prudential logo, with its new face of 'Prudence'. Some £1 million was invested in designing and establishing this logo, culminating in a major PR affair at the Royalty Theatre. Some people argued in advance that Prudence would make Prudential the laughing stock of the City. Wolff Olins, the major designer who had developed her, managed to convince the board otherwise.

The difficulty with corporate logos is that they have to last. US designer Saul Bass, whose Los Angeles company Bass Yager has developed such major trademarks as those of Quaker Oats, Warner Communications, and AT&T, insists that 'the logo must not only express what the company is, but what it will become'. This is all the more important in these days when a Hanson Trust can come up behind you and overnight change your company's identity or, at any rate, structure.

What exactly makes a good corporate logo is even more difficult to define. Think of Penguin. Think more recently of the Diana figure used by the new publishing firm, Bloomsbury. Such figures are highly sophisticated in the way they evoke powerful associations relevant to their company, rather than providing direct information in the manner of a lavatory sign.

Whatever you have to package – product or company – it is virtually essential nowadays that you use good design. In some cases, it is vital because packaging will be the only point-of-sale aid you have. Of course, there are dangers here. Designers and design groups can be very expensive. You pay them in hourly rates, depending on the number of personnel working on your project, and who knows how many hours it takes to produce a great design? It can take one man one hour – a freak occurrence – or a team of 10 people ten weeks and more. But the risks are worth taking.

Desk research – exactly what its name implies – is where you should always begin your search for consumer and product understanding. It will involve looking through published information, such as government statistics, trade publications and market reports. It is cheap and will help you to clarify your ideas for more detailed analysis later. Its limitations are that it is extremely time consuming (unless you have a department of research assistants working for you) and the nature of the information is such that it is generally available to your competitors as well.

One area of desk research which is often underrated, although it is unlikely to be available to competitors, is the statistical information provided by your own company. Re-marshalled and intelligently interpreted it can provide insights of startling clarity, sometimes into where products have gone wrong.

Quantitative and qualitative research differ from desk research in that it is tailor-made for particular marketing situations. Its complexity and labour intensity are such that it is usually farmed out to specialist market research consultancies, which do not come cheap.

Quantitative research is designed to elicit how many people and what sort of people buy, or would like to buy, particular products. Qualitative research is interested in why people like, or dislike, products. It will be quickly spotted that quantitative research has affinities with demographics, while qualitative research leans towards motivational psychology. Over the years a rather barren controversy has sprung up among market research specialists over such issues as whether qualitative research can ever stand on its own as a decision-making platform without being validated by quantitative research.

This book cannot presume to sit in judgement on such issues. However, it may be said that qualitative research is now more widely used than ever before and tends to be of most use in the area of 'soft data', including attitudes, opinions, imagery and belief, where qualitative research is relatively disadvantaged.

Sampling

Both methods of research rely upon the same underlying principle: that it is possible to determine what a great many people think or do by exploring the responses of a small sample of them. Sampling, if it is to be an accurate reflection of the market, relies upon two vital premises. First, that those people interviewed tell the truth. By and large this has been found to be the case, so long as the questions concern themselves with matters of fact rather than opinion. The second premise is that the sample must be representative of what is called the *universe* of product users (ie, all of them); if not, all the research findings are invalidated. Obviously, the ideal sample would be the complete universe of a chosen target group, but prohibitive expense and logistics rule this out. Generally, the bigger the sample the more accurate the findings and the more expensive the survey.

There are two ways to select a sample for quantitative research: *quota sampling* and *random probability*. In the case of quota sampling, the researcher first determines the nature of the target universe by applying geo-demographic criteria, and then finds an agreed sample size of people matching this profile who are interviewed with a set questionnaire.

Quota sampling is cheaper, but less reliable than random probability. Here a complete list of the universe is drawn up – such as an electoral register from a certain district – and a set percentage of names are selected at random. The interviewer then makes every effort to interview the selected names (with the same set of questions), sometimes returning time and time again to the same house until he gets a result. At first sight this might seem pedantic. Why not interview a next-door neighbour if the person you have selected is persistently out? In fact it will become apparent after a moment's thought that the person who is out may have very different behavioural patterns from the person who is usually at home.

One-off surveys, or groups of surveys of this sort, which are designed to elicit specific information about a particular product or type of consumer are known as *ad hoc* research. Very often, however, an accurate picture of a market can only be pieced together by longer term or *continuous* research. This is generally conducted by the large research companies, such as AC Neilsen and AGB, by means of permanent *panels* or *audits*.

Neilsen, in particular, is the most widely accepted source of continuous research on retail sales audits in FMCG markets (particularly beverages and groceries) in the UK. Every two months a host of Neilsen executives descend on a wide sample of retailers who have agreed to let them analyse in minute detail, levels of stock, goods being sold, market shares and the average prices of goods. Technology is helping to speed up this process through the use of such devices as bar coding and holograms.

An alternative method of monitoring consumer behaviour (and finding out what happens in those shops which are not a part of the retail audit) is to set up panels of consumers who supply the research company with a diary of their purchases (or the labels from them) every week. The resulting reports are then sold to subscribers and act as a kind of tracking study of consumer behaviour.

Halfway between these extremes of *ad hoc* and continuous research are what is known as *omnibus* surveys. These are conducted regularly but involve certain specific questions. It is a way of sharing the costs of *ad hoc* research between several clients.

Qualitative research tends to involve less formal questions, with smaller samples. It relies for its effectiveness upon more highly trained interviewers who conduct much lengthier interviews. The end product is a series of recorded quotations, rather than a series of statistics.

The two standard methods of conducting qualitative research are group discussions and the so-called semi-structured interview. Group discussions, the more widely used of the two, are likely to involve between 4 and 12 interviewees who represent the target market – be it housewives, vegetarians or dog owners – and who will be cross-examined for about two hours by the interviewer. Normally the exact name of the commissioning client is kept a secret to exclude bias.

Semi-structured interviews mean in effect in-depth

interviews with individuals, where a group discussion is likely to be an inhibiting environment.

Case History No 3. Market Research: The Launch and Relaunch of *The Mail on Sunday*

In 1980/81 Associated Newspapers were very keen to launch another Sunday title. There were two big unknowns which research had to verify – the extent of consumer demand for a new Sunday paper, and the length of time it would take to establish consumer loyalty.

The Sunday market had long been stagnant, even declining, but Associated Newspapers thought there was a gap in the middle sector. Wary of the cost of failure, they used research to identify the right readership profile, and how to reach it.

Qualitative research using group discussions showed a high level of interest in a 'Sunday equivalent of the *Daily Mail* ', which became the positioning. Target readers were defined as *Daily Mail* readers and younger ABC1s, both readers and non-readers of other Sunday newspapers.

Associated Newspapers knew it was crucial for success in terms of advertising revenue to deliver a readership profile of at least 55 per cent ABC1s in the paper's first year. Further research, in the form of a DOE survey, showed that these people rise and shop later on Sundays than C2DEs, and might get to newsagents when copies had been sold out. So it was important to encourage ABC1 readers to order delivered copies. A *Daily Mail* promotion was developed offering *Mail* readers a discount on ordered copies. A total of 450,000 orders were placed, the largest advance order ever for a new paper. But due to poor quality product, initial sales of the paper were well short of the 1.25m sales target.

Previous research had been around concepts rather than dummies (specimen issues) of the paper, which made it difficult for interviewees to articulate what they wanted. New research with copies of the real paper elicited much more useful reactions, and the paper was radically revised in line with the findings. Four supplements were added, enabling the whole family to read a section of the paper simultaneously.

Sales went up quite radically on relaunch, from 800,000 to 1.25 million from the first week. Eventually, the paper stabilised at a circulation of 1.3 million, right on target.

Test marketing

You have got your product. You have done your research on the target market and are satisfied with the results. You have positioned the product, named it, given it a brand identity and decided what the packaging is going to look like. But before you commit millions of pounds (in all probability) to a national launch, you have one last chance to probe the consumer's views and make any necessary modifications: the test market.

Test markets, which take, if you like, a sample of the national market, are used for a variety of purposes. Their function is to test not only the response to new products, but allow for modifications to old ones, such as pricing and packaging, or as British Telecom did for a couple of years, find out which types of advertising campaign elicited the most positive response.

Test marketing is, of course, a very expensive item in the armoury of the marketing department. Yet to pull a product at the test market stage represents only a small fraction of the cost of a national flop. And sometimes the costs can be extremely low. TSW can put an advertisement on television for a cost of £10,000, and provide a range of support services, which will, according to TSW contractor, Pauline Shuker, be at least a workmanlike job.

As this indicates, products can be tested at a variety of levels. At the simplest, your product is likely to be tested 'blind' by a panel of consumers who will be able to compare it with a number of existing competitors. At its most complex the aim will be to create a microcosm of the national market environment.

This will include placing the product in retail outlets in certain test markets, and backing the product with an advertising budget probably over a period of several months. Many

television areas can provide guaranteed distribution and easy
link-ups with retailers. Tyne Tees offers listings for grocery,
drink and DIY brands through Argyll, the Co-Op, Morrisons
and Walter Wilson. Anglia attracts a wide range of drinks brands
because it has an agreement with Peter Dominic. Such
agreements are very attractive to advertisers because limited test
distribution can otherwise be difficult to arrange.

If successful in test the product can then be launched
nationally. If it has only been modestly successful you can try a
second test market to clarify the position, or to explore the
possibility of fine-tuning the product.

One problem with the test market is that it is never an exact
indication of national behaviour. Although, for example, you can
use television advertising locally, you cannot use the press in
quite the same way (unless of course you were only planning to
use local press advertising). Some marketing directors go even
further and argue that the concept of a television test area as a
microcosm of the nation is totally out-of-date. Television test
areas, they believe, offer suitable rather than typical profiles,
TVS being an excellent example. It is becoming more and more
popular as a test area despite its untypical profile, being noted
for its significant numbers of affluent ABs.

Another thing to watch is your competitors, especially if your
test market has a long gestation period. Once they find out, they
may bias results by pouring more of their own resources into the
test area. Worse still, you have now irrevocably moved away
from product secrecy. They may spot your product's unique
benefit and exploit it by beating you to the national launch with a
rival product.

Test marketing can often be very helpful in revealing new
information about a product. Brillo's Instant Shoe Shine is a
case in point. The company needed to jettison its one-product
reputation, but not in such a way that it would antagonise the big
guns in the household cleaning market, Proctor and Gamble,
Lever Brothers and Colgate Palmolive. Its solution was to test
market a number of new products in small niche markets where
there had been little innovation, and advertising support for
existing products had fallen away.

One of these new products was Instant Shoe Shine. It used a technical innovation, the silicone-impregnated sponge, which does not clean shoes but imports a shine without fuss. It was positioned in a stagnant market with two well-known but largely unsupported brands, Kiwi and Cherry Blossom. Other companies had tried the silicone sponge concept, but in the opinion of Brillo's marketing department they had either overpriced or failed to explain it sufficiently to the consumer. So Brillo aimed to give it full advertising support in the test market.

The test market chosen was the Tyne Tees Television area, where Instant Shoe Shine was supported with a £250,000 campaign. The results showed that it had achieved far better than expected distribution, but – and this was the fascinating revelation – it had hardly touched the traditional shoecare market. Its results were incremental to the market, in other words it had found totally new customers. The total market went up 50 per cent with Brillo's share by value at 32 per cent, Cherry Blossom at 28 per cent and Kiwi at 22 per cent.

The new product was rolled out a few months later in the Granada, Yorkshire, Wales and TSW areas with a similar, weighted, advertising budget. The results broadly echoed those of the original test market. As a result, Brillo then launched Instant Shoe Shine nationally.

Example

Market Research Questionnaire
Here is part of a typical research questionnaire designed to elicit detailed responses to different product features.

Q.14
I am about to show you some ranges of packs for different brands of hair conditioner and read out some comments other people have made about them. Please tell me, as I do so, judging by how the packs of each range appear to you, to which of the ranges of packs each comment applies. You may feel a comment applies to all ranges or to just some or to none at all.
Allow respondent time to view all brands

Q.15

First of all which of these packs do you personally think look ...
(read out below)

	A	B	C	D	E	F	All of them.
Up-to-date, modern							
Rather ordinary							
Gimmicky							
Feminine							
Not for me							
Glamorous							
Poor value for money							
Distinctive							

	A	B	C	D	E	F	All of them
Expensive looking							
Easy to handle							

Q.16

Which of the packs looks as if it would contain a conditioner
which would ...
(read out below)

	A	B	C	D	E	F	All of them	None of them
Be different								

*Be really good
for your hair*

*Have a fresh and
natural perfume*

Be a high quality

*Be made with
good ingredients*

*Will leave hair
looking really nice*

Q.17

I will read out some descriptions of several different people or
personalities who use conditioner. For each description, please
tell me just by looking at each of the ranges, which ones you
think would most likely be used by.... You may give as many as
you like for each range.
(read out below)

	A	B	C	D	E	F	All of them
A young teenage girl							
An older woman							
A price-conscious person							
A lively, youthful male							
A young woman							
A working woman							
Men as well as women							
Anyone in the family							

Part II: Strategy

Once the marketing manager has analysed his products, their strengths and shortcomings, and the market for those products, both actual and potential, he must now form a marketing plan. That plan will have to embrace how the products should be developed, if at all, and how they should reach their market.

Ideally it should be carefully organised, balancing different strategies within the total product mix, and different media within the media mix. In practice, marketing plans are often ad hoc affairs, thrown together in response to other managers within the company or to market pressures outside the company. If there is a definite marketing plan, it can be a once-a-year ritual which is then quietly shelved and forgotten. The company does not sufficiently respect either the need for marketing or the importance of the marketing manager. That attitude, though, is changing. Let us assume for the time being that there is time and opportunity to plan carefully.

4
Developing the Product

Existing products

The first question which you normally have to consider when establishing a marketing plan is whether to develop the product. Should it be modified? Should the range of products be extended? Do you need to introduce or innovate a new product altogether?

But can the existing product be improved? Can it be made more effective – faster, longer-lasting, tougher, less fattening, heavy, expensive, or whatever? Can the product be made to do more? Can the washing powder be made to tackle more stains, the car be given more features? While most products usually can be improved, it is not always worth the cost involved.

Can the range of products be extended? Can a new flavour be added to your range of cereals, a new colour to your paints, a new model to your cars? Again, in Britain as opposed to America, where the range of products is sometimes too great if anything, there are usually possibilities for extra variety. Even with a Coca-Cola, there is a possibility for Tab, or a Cherry Coke.

It is also worth considering whether the range should actually be cut down. Many producers are finding in today's highly professional world that the pressure is to specialise and rationalise. Hence you will find a major company such as United Biscuits cutting out brands like Granola and Royal Scot to concentrate on its main brand, McVities.

When major food retailing figure John Fletcher took over confectionery firm Barker and Dobson, he also took similar action. He found a company with lines of sweets that were not

51

selling particularly well in their own right, and plant that was not sufficiently cost-effective to produce own-brand confectionery for others. So he followed a policy of acquisition and rationalisation and ended up eliminating Barker and Dobson, and concentrated on producing own-brand confectionery for Tesco. This was found to be much more profitable then producing for smaller retailers.

One alternative, if a product is not selling well, may be to repackage it not just slightly, but entirely, and give it a totally new identity. This is what happened with Biarritz, the new, distinctive, triangle-shaped box of chocolates, launched recently. Actually, the chocolates inside are not new. Biarritz was a response to the fact that consumers felt standard boxes of chocolates were rather out-of-date, with associations of being middle-aged and greedy. They were like so many jewel cases, romantic perhaps, but in the style of the 1950s and *Come Dancing*. Now women want something that has style. Biarritz satisfies this need. Its triangle shape is novel and modern, and has been very successful.

If you are looking for positive variations on the existing product, the case of Cherry Pepsi illustrates one important principle in new product development – always start with a clear strategy and benefit in mind. Pepsi had a strategy to begin with. They wanted to offer a cola alternative to the teenagers who are so important to the soft drinks market.

That was when the technicians were brought in. Several questions were asked including: What flavours have the same type of profile as cola, and yet are different? How many of them are dark in colour? How many have a good flavour in both sucrose and non-sucrose syrups? Each further question helped eliminate more and more possible alternatives so that in the end the decision was obvious.

Another interesting case is that of Bisto Sauce Granules. Following the success of its Bisto Gravy Granules RHM looked for another product to utilise its existing plant. It actually considered a wide variety of product concepts as varied as hot drinks and puddings, before identifying a distinct opportunity for sauces.

A number of product prototypes and packaging formats were considered. One idea early on was to produce a base sauce, to which you could add ingredients to make other sauces. Research showed this was not popular. Who wanted to fry onions to make onion sauce? Most housewives would rather leave the sauce out of the meal altogether.

In the end the researchers arrived at the only slightly more complex concept of Bisto Sauce Granules, a range of three popular sauces – cheese, parsley and white. An important part of the concept was packaging them in a Bisto Gravy Granules drum, which appealed to housewives who resented having to waste sauce when not using a whole sachet.

Thus a very successful extension of an original concept was developed, helping to extend the Bisto name away from its gravy past.

Many new product ideas are, like Bisto Sauces, essentially a repackaging or recombining of existing products. A striking example is the recent mould-breaking introduction of the Phileas Fogg range of adult snacks. Until then, it had been assumed that snacks were essentially childish in their appeal, there could be little real product differentiation, and that prices had to be low.

What Derwent Valley Foods, manufacturer of the new range, did was to take a range of good, previously rather different products, and bring them together under a new 'umbrella' aimed at adults and priced at a premium. The success of this £10 million brand has excited the admiration of many marketing managers.

New products

What may be needed is an entirely new product. The reason, as we have already seen, is that ultimately all products die, and all companies along with them, unless they keep innovating. The major corporations which have survived for any length of time, such as IBM, have done so precisely because they were able to keep coming up with new ideas.

But the invention of new products and innovation of new

services must be treated with extreme caution. It is easy for marketing managers and other departments to be swept away with enthusiasm for new product ideas, and for the costs of research consequently to balloon out of all proportion to initial estimates, as more and more tests and investigations are called for.

Every new product idea must be examined in relation to the company's capabilities. Does it fit in with and enhance existing products, or is it totally out of character, like a new washing powder for a car manufacturer? Can the production line or factory actually produce it? Can the sales force sell it? Above all, can it actually be produced at a price that will attract customers, for a cost that will yield a profit?

Of course, it is all very well rejecting ideas, but first you have to find them. The important point here is that the research and development department is not the only source of ideas. There can be many other valuable contributors to the creative process. All the various departments in the company should be consulted, including production, engineering and sales. Any one of them may have ideas that have occurred to the back-room boys precisely because they are looking at the product in a different environment and in a different way.

Customers too should be consulted. They may have simple desires, requests and needs, both for changes regarding existing products and for new products, which have not yet come to your attention. Competitors can be another valuable source of ideas. They may be trying, and failing to develop some new product, which your company might be able to bring to realisation, or they may be just about to introduce something new.

Competitors should be interpreted loosely. Look at general usage of similar products and related services. Individual tea-bags on a tag, for example, have been used in the catering world for ages. But it was only recently that Brooke Bond thought of taking the idea into the retail sector. The result was PG Tags which in just a year has claimed between 1 per cent and 1.5 per cent of the national tea market.

Other sources of ideas are government agencies and educational institutions, which are often teeming with unexploited ideas. Such cooperation, between government, education, and industry is worth examining since in many countries it is still in its infancy. You can also approach new product development consultants for ideas. Being specialists they are usually not only creative but have a variety of structured techniques for producing ideas.

One favoured technique is the Synectics method of brain-storming, which lays great stress on developing rather than attacking the suggestions of participants, and thus encouraging creativity. Another method commonly used involves building a three-dimensional model of a market in order to identify gaps. Next analyse competing brands in terms of different dimensions – the toilet cleaner market, for example, in terms of price, powder/liquid, odour and germ-killing ability. Thus was born the fragrant and deadly Frish.

The Reckitt and Colman Pharmaceutical Division came up with a somewhat similar solution by a different route. They used research to find out people's attitudes to Dettol and similar cleaning products. Analysis showed that an increasing number of people were prepared to accept that germ killing could be effective without the reassurance of a strong functional smell. This was very important in the kitchen where the need to kill germs without odour or tainting was paramount. Thus they arrived at Dettox – a clear, fresh, no-perfume disinfectant cleaner.

NPD Consultancy, Presight, used one very interesting and fruitful method of idea generation – which can be applied to a whole range of problems – they asked housewives to keep a dishwashing diary. They found out that nearly everybody had problems getting glasses clean, and even had special methods of dealing with them, such as cleaning them first, or getting their husbands to stand by ready to polish. Thus was born the idea of a special washing-up liquid for glasses.

Perhaps the most important method of all for having ideas is quantity, for the more ideas you produce, the better your chance of having a good one. Great ideas may even arrive in a miraculous flash, but only after a lot of hard work.

Case History No. 4. New Product Development: Solmin

Reckitt and Colman Pharmaceuticals gave new product development company Craton Lodge and Knight the brief of developing a major new analgesic, that would be significantly different from their existing Disprin brand, but not destroy its sales.

CLK quickly established that the analgesic market was extremely crowded and therefore if a brand was to be successful it had to be based on a clear consumer, rather than manufacturer benefit. A magical new formula in itself would not guarantee success. From the analysis of several development stages which considered various product, pack and concept presentations, three key areas emerged. One concerned portability, another the ease of taking the tablet since headaches often occur when people are on the move or in public places where it is impossible to obtain a glass of water.

These areas were exploited in the product form of Solmin – a tablet which dissolved in the mouth without water, and in the packaging – a portable tube designed to be kept in the pocket or handbag.

The third benefit of the Solmin was a special screwing action for the cap. One danger pharmaceutical manufacturers must consider is that of tablets getting into the hands of young children, who may end up eating them like sweets. So CLK developed and patented a special screwing action to defeat children but not adults.

Solmin was test marketed in the Yorkshire region in 1983, where it achieved all its targets. Susequently, it was marketed nationally and has since become a major brand.

Some companies are highly creative in their own right, an obvious example being IDV, (International Distillers and Vintners). IDV has managed to develop a notable reputation for product development in a field where there is intense competition and interest in building huge, international brands. Since the early 1970s IDV can number among its creations Piat d'Or wine, Bailey's Irish Cream, Malibu coconut liqueur and Croft

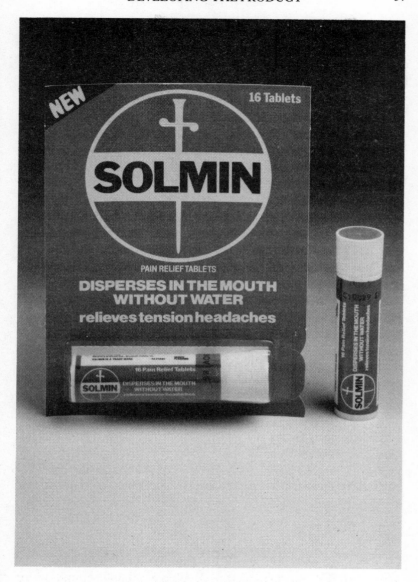

Original pale cream sherry. It has exploited the fact that consumers have been losing their taste for traditional liqueurs, and titillated them with more exotic flavours and combinations. (Piat d'Or, it must be revealed, is actually a rather sweet German style of wine masquerading as a sophisticated French brand).

IDV's success has meant that whereas seven or eight years ago it was almost the only company innovating in the field, there have been between 300 and 400 new drinks launches in the past three years alone.

5
Planning Promotion

Promotional budget

Once you have your products, it is very tempting to rush straight in with ideas for promoting them. But can you afford them? Therefore, the first action you have to take involves working out your promotional budget, or your *appropriation*. Once you have established that, you can work out a *marketing mix*, how you are going to distribute that budget between promotions in different media and through different channels.

There are various formulae followed for working out the appropriation, but none of them should be treated as law since there are no laws concerning the effectiveness of advertising and promotion. Each formula has its own advantages and disadvantages.

What one can say about them is that they tend to fall into two camps, conservative and progressive. The conservative formulae are based mainly on *existing* sales, the progressive formulae look forward to sales *targets*. Which particular formula you choose is going to be very much a matter of your own temperament and situation.

Two closely related conservative formulae are *percentage of last year's turnover* and *percentage of last year's profits*. Here you look at last year's results and either allocate a set percentage of turnover to this year's promotion, or take a percentage of profits, deducting a certain amount for research and development. The advantage of this approach is that it is very safe for you are only spending what is in the kitty. The disadvantage is that it is static and unambitious. It leaves very little room for major expansion.

A much more progressive approach is to work out the

anticipated turnover this year, and allow a percentage of that for promotion. The advantage of this approach is that it does make for growth. The disadvantage is that it can be dangerous if you get your figures totally wrong. Sales might go down instead of up.

Another approach is that of *marginal revenue*. This simply means that if the marginal revenue produced by advertising, ie. the extra sales minus the extra costs, is greater than the cost of advertising, you will make a profit enabling you to advertise. The disadvantage of this approach is that the effects of advertising are not always immediately obvious. Decisions to purchase may be delayed rather than instant, and advertising which is effective in the long run may seem unprofitable in the short term.

One approach to determining the appropriation that is neither conservative nor progressive but somewhere in the middle, is that of considering *competitors' expenditure*. You look at how much your fiercest competitor, or your average competitor, is spending pro rata on his products, and you match him. The problem here is that competitors may be spending illogically. The market may be overcrowded.

All formulae go out of the window when you are promoting a new product. Then the initial costs may be extremely high, as much as 25 per cent of sales, on the calculation that once the product is established promotional activity can be considerably reduced.

How you choose between these and other formulae is very much down to your personal disposition and company's situation. The important point is to be clear about what formula or approach you are following and, at the same time, to be flexible and prepared to introduce variations.

The Authors' group came up with an interesting variation on the marginal revenue formula, when it was asked to pitch for a large £1m plus account by a major insurance and investment group. Various products and services, including insurance and unit trusts, would have to be advertised, so, according to the brief, there would be no money for television. Nevertheless, Moorgate felt that a group of this size really needed television both for prestige and to help sales through intermediaries. It suggested that the group devote £700,000 of the budget to advertising a single pension plan off-the-page in major national daily newspapers. They calculated this would yield nearly £3m for the group in the way of commissions and would pay for television advertising, which they also proposed. The client did not in the end follow the plan, but they gave Moorgate the account!

Media mix

Having worked out a budget, the marketing manager can now get down to the media mix – that is, how he will divide up the money for promotion between different media and the means of reaching the market.

A natural question which many people pose is whether it is necessary to promote or advertise at all. Can a product not be sold exclusively by salesmen? Some products perhaps, especially the more complex, industrial ones. But the counter-question in this instance is: can salesmen reach all the people who make the buying decisions, and indeed all the people who influence buying decisions? The person who actually chooses that photocopier may have been influenced in the first place by a whole range of people from the managing director down to the secretaries and office juniors who are continually complaining about the existing copiers. It is very rare, in fact, for salesmen to reach all the key figures, or reach them profitably. Salesmen, it must be remembered, can be very expensive per customer. Usually you have to promote your products.

Next you have to look at the merits of the different media available. Are you going to commit everything to a massive television campaign (massive by your budget)? Are you going to distribute the money evenly between various media? Are you going to plump for a direct mail campaign alone? Or, as the cynic might put it, if you have barely enough money for advertising, should you concentrate on public relations?

In making a choice, there are various criteria you can apply. The first criterion comes from answering the question: What is the *audience* of a given medium, and how closely does it approximate to your target market? Then you have to ask: What is the *cost* of reaching that market per reader/viewer/listener? Next, the very important questions: How *measurable* are the results of your advertising or promotional activities in a given medium? And: How sure can you be that you have actually reched your target market?

The other criteria that must be applied when considering various media concern their suitability for your product. Probably the most important question is what are its *powers of reproduction*? How close is the image presented to the real object? How excitingly is the product conveyed? What is the ambience of the medium? Does it add excitement, glamour, or does it detract from the product?

Next you have to look at the *complexity* of the medium and the product. In other words, is this particular medium able to convey all the benefits of your product? In practice, however, you can only present a few of a product's many features when advertising or promoting it.

Finally, you have to look at the *prestige* of a particular medium. Is this the right place for your product to be seen? Is the medium going to help upgrade or degrade your product in the public's eyes? These are not the only criteria that you can apply in choosing media but they are probably the most important.

When applying these criteria do remember that there is always a case for taking the unconventional route. A product may stand out precisely because it is in the 'wrong' place, yielding excellent sales results. Radio, for example, was hardly an obvious choice for Kotex Simplicity Towels. At that time women's magazines had been the main medium for advertising sanitary protection, and had clear advantages including colour advertisements and the right environment.

However, the advertising agency Leo Burnett wanted to do something unexpected in order to make its advertising stand out. It considered commercial radio, arguing that it could make significant tonal contributions of music and voice. It could reach women at certain times in the day when they alone were listening, offering one-to-one communication. It had a young audience, and was a young medium, and therefore would help update the image of Simplicity Towels.

So a radio campaign was developed involving rock and disco music, and describing days out when sudden delays meant women had to stay out longer but without problems, thanks to Simplicity. Research showed a major increase in brand awareness and confidence as a result of this advertising and, most important of all, sales in areas where radio was used were significantly higher than non-radio areas.

Advertising

Television

This is the most popular medium, attracting massive audiences, although you have to be careful because audiences can vary by as much as 50 per cent between one commercial break and another, and by a similar figure between one programme in a series and the next. There is always a certain risk in taking television time because you do not know how popular the Royal programme will be that evening. Also, in certain cases, you may not even know exactly what programme is going to accompany your commercial, for it may not be announced until near the showing date.

The television audience is very much a captive one, even in these days of channel 'zapping' and quick rushes to the kitchen during the breaks. But if they are watching, then your commercial is liable to occupy their senses.

Also television can be extremely expensive. To run a national campaign nowadays can cost £800,000, and a 30-second spot on Thames Television between 6.30 and 8.30 in the evening can cost £20,000. Recently, the costs of television time have been spiralling, rising in an 18-month period by 25 per cent, over 4 times the rise of inflation. Major advertisers have been complaining furiously. Even so, the big spenders such as Rowntree-Mackintosh, Cadbury, Brooke Bond Oxo and Procter and Gamble will still spend 90 per cent of their budgets on television, though some are being forced to cut back on the number of products they advertise.

On the other hand, television need not be that expensive. If you have the right region, as we saw with TSW, you can put out a campaign for as little as £10,000. It also helps to place television commercials carefully at low-cost times, when programmes such as *The Money Programme* or DIY/consumer programmes, which attract specialist audiences, are running. Both caution and optimism have to be exercised in considering television.

Of course, what attracts everyone to television are its powers of reproduction. It is so lifelike, offering movement, sound and colour, and it can add tremendous excitement. Nothing else, apart from cinema, can match it in conveying the experience of a product – the thrill of driving a car, the awe of flying by plane, the sensuousness of soap and cosmetic products.

There is no question that these powers work and sell products. There are countless cases of products being sold out after being advertised on television. Confectionery items are the classic examples, but there are many others.

The campaign for Steradent Deep Clean denture cleaner shows television's superior sales power in certain instances very clearly. This was a fast-acting denture cleaner. The target market was loosely described as the over 35s, although in fact four out of five of those with false teeth are over 45. The Deep Clean campaign embraced both national press and regional television in Lancashire and Yorkshire. Right from the start, sales in those two regions far outpaced the rest of the country. Sales increased at double the rate of the rest of the country in Lancashire, and were 50 per cent higher in Yorkshire.

In the USA, the world's Number 1 stockbroker Merrill Lynch turned to television when other measures had failed to produce sufficient sales of a £1 billion mutual fund, (or 'unit trust' in our language). The fund sold out in a few days. Television can also create sudden and remarkable shifts in attitudes as well as sales. Brylcreem is one case in point. Here was a product used predominantly by people over 55. Research showed that people aged 30 to 45 favoured 'natural look' hair, but that 15 to 29 year olds tended to prefer a 'fashion look'. So there was a potential gap in the market.

Three commercials were developed which took nostalgic and traditional 1960s Brylcreem advertising and modernised it. These were then broadcast in London, the fashion centre of Britain.

Immediately after the advertising stopped a quantitative attitude dipstick survey was conducted among 15 to 24 year-old males on the telephone to assess the advertising's effects. The survey showed that there was an 84 per cent awareness in London, while in the Central Television region the figure was just 30 per cent. Further questions showed that perceptions of the brand had completely changed to the extent that Brylcreem was now seen as positively fashionable.

Case History No 5. The Power of Television: Datacopy

Datacopy provides a fascinating example of television's power to sell and also change attitudes in the process, and how it can be used to advertise even apparently complex products. Datacopy is a revolutionary new copying paper, which is even-sided and therefore goes through the photocopier with much less friction, making jamming a far less common occurrence.

Research undertaken by advertising agency Yellowhammer showed that some 70 per cent of office workers regard trouble-free photocopying as a priority, and jamming as a major cause of aggravation. Yellowhammer proposed the revolutionary step of turning to television. It argued that with a wide subsidiary target audience of office workers involved in photocopying, from the office junior to – in small companies – the chairman, Datacopy was a very consumer-orientated product.

It was decided that the core target audience should be the personnel managers in companies responsible for dealing with suppliers, predominantly ABC1 business persons. Yellow-hammer developed a 30-second commercial humorously

dramatising what happens when the office photocopier gets jammed and an engineer has to be called. LWT was chosen as the first station because of its high returns of upmarket viewers. It was decided to reach decision-makers at the weekend, when there was a good chance they would be watching television. Channel 4 was used predominantly, with advertising mainly during current affairs, sports and business programmes.

The launch campaign ran for four weeks with remarkable and surprising results. In addition to creating massive awareness of the product among the target audience, television had a knock-on effect among stockists and employees, who all now wanted to be associated with the product.

The success of the initial campaign led to it being shown in most other regions. One year after launch Datacopy had become the second largest brand of copying paper to Rank Xerox with a 12 per cent share of a market worth £125 million. The many doubters and critics who thought that television was totally the wrong medium for a product such as Datacopy were completely disproven.

It has to be remembered though, that television is very much a transient medium. If your commercial does not create a memorable image, it can easily be forgotten in the hours between its presentation and shopping. Television commercials cannot be retained, reexamined and studied like newspaper advertisements. This is particularly significant when you are aiming at an older market because older people tend to have a much lower recall of commercials.

Above all, television is not very good at presenting complex products. Commercials can only and should only present one or two benefits of a product quickly and powerfully – the viewer cannot really retain more information. (Some commercials for *The Sun* in recent years were exceptions in that they crammed as many features of the next week's papers as they could into 30 seconds or a minute. But what was retained in the viewer's mind was not so much specific attractions of the next week, as the general impression of an 'action-packed' paper, and that was what kept attracting new readers and boosting the paper's circulation.) The normal simplicity of television commercials attracts the inevitable accusation of simplification, particularly when advertising political or financial matters. Television is not good for presenting the intricate benefits of something like an insurance plan.

This does not mean that you cannot present complex products at all on television, for financial advertisers are turning to television in even greater numbers, but they are using it in tandem with other media. The television campaign for Legal & General, for example, points people to their financial adviser to back up their claims. Other campaigns will ask people to look at the advertisements in their daily paper.

One of the financial pioneers in television was stockbroking firm Capel-Cure Myers. It used a television campaign partly to promote its corporate identity, partly to promote the Master Portfolio Service, which requires a minimum initial investment of £50,000 – hardly the sort of product you would think suited to television.

A 40-second commercial was developed and run on LWT with the aim of reaching a target audience of ABC1 adults. The campaign was heavily slanted towards the cheaper rates of Channel 4, concentrating on high-yielding ABC1 programmes such as *The Business Programme*, sport, documentaries, and Friday's *News at Ten*. Although Capel felt that it might take up to one year for the campaign to reshape its corporate identity, the company was delighted with the initial results. It found there was a marked increase in enquiries for its services after the commercials were shown.

Where television also scores very heavily is in terms of prestige. 'As advertised on TV' is an automatic credential for any product. By contrast, other media have far less prestige. No one makes the claim, for example, 'as advertised through your letterbox' for products promoted through direct mail.

Television clearly lent prestige to a small Devon-based company AGS Home Improvements, which was having trouble convincing houseowners that it was a reputable outfit. It sells and installs replacement windows and doors in a market plagued by cowboys. Exmouth advertising agency, Tony Corbett, produced a £40,000 television campaign which was transmitted on TSW, depicting AGS as a local, honest, family-owned firm, with good quality products and reliable service, and firmly avoiding any attempt to sell on low price. The results were soon measurable. AGS door-to-door sales staff were met with much warmer receptions, and sales were up 31 per cent on the previous year.

Press

The press reaches almost the entire UK population, with nearly everyone reading one of the major morning newspapers. Most people, in fact, read two of the Sunday newspapers published in London. Most adults read an evening newspaper. We are a very literate country.

The different papers offer an immense variety of target audiences, all the way from the multimillion circulation of *The Sun* and *Mirror* to the multi-thousand readership of a local paper or specialist magazine. Thanks to the National Readership Survey, detailed readership data are available for about 90 of these publications. Many of them, particularly some magazines, offer very specialist readerships. If you are selling an 'add-on' for an Amstrad computer, obviously one of the various Amstrad computer magazines gives you direct access to a quality audience. Similarly, the local paper may be invaluable to the local shopkeeper.

A combination of different publications should enable you to reach your target audience, but the question is at what cost? The press is probably one of the cheapest media, but you have to be careful. The more select a publication's readership the more you usually have to pay, and sometimes the costs can be exorbitant. A magazine such as *Punch* may charge a premium price for advertisements, while delivering a stagnant circulation and steadily declining readership. You may find that even for some up-market products, a relatively cheap, popular paper such as *The Star* may offer better value than the premium-priced quality papers.

The press can be an excellent way of extending your market. The most successful direct-mail users, for example, are likely to find that they reach a point where the universe of direct-mailing lists is exhausted. In the end there may simply be no more names to be tested, but press advertisements can elicit new customers.

The drawback of advertising in some papers is that they have poor black and white reproduction. Those offering colour reproduction can provide an enormous impact, especially within the context of otherwise grey papers, but they may be too expensive. Your choice here depends to a great extent on how important reproduction is to the sales of your product.

Magazines, on the other hand, can offer more impact than even television because their detail is that much finer. Some foods will look more appetising in magazines, some perfume bottles more elegant, some clothes more stylish. In addition, the still photograph may have certain advantages over television in that, being still, it is better suited to a mythic treatment of products, with more being left to the imagination. One example is the long-running campaign for Marlboro cigarettes which, through photographs, has recreated a mythical world of rugged cowboys.

The press is much better than television for presenting complex products and services. The copywriter who has previously had to hone copy down to one or two measly benefits occupying a few lines on the page of a script, is suddenly faced with relative acres of space. He can take his time leading the reader through the product's virtues, provided the headline and visual have first grabbed the reader's attention. But space is not entirely limitless.

Many publications lend prestige to advertisers. The readers tend to presume that a newspaper or magazine stands behind the products advertised in its pages but this is not always the case. So the press may sometimes be imperative for a new, unknown advertiser. But as with all media, it is important to check that your advertisement fits the publication selected. An advertisement for a Rolls Royce is unlikely to do well in *The Mirror*.

The press is an excellent medium if you want to sell direct, off-the-page, and a single advertisement for a financial product can attract hundreds of thousands of pounds from investors. The press also allows for flexibility. You can change your advertising campaign, or the size of your advertisements and the papers you use as results start to come in. (Television, it is true, can be used for direct response advertising – to sell records, for example, or elicit money for charities. But it is a costly method because if the advice of expert direct marketers is to be followed, you have to leave the company's name and address on the screen at the end for about 15 seconds to give people time to write them down. You have a considerable expense before you have even started to sell the product.)

It is often difficult to calculate the precise impact of a press campaign. The Anadin press campaign in Scotland, however, is a clear success story. The following Case History relates the story behind the decision for a campaign and explains why it was a success.

Case History No 6. The power of the press: Anadin

Anadin's venture into mixed media proved so sucessful that David Beauchamp, Marketing Director and Roy Bookman, Group Marketing Manager of Whitehall Laboratories, were delighted to relate the whole story to Torin Douglas.

Torin Douglas: What led you to put Anadin into a mixed media test?

David Beauchamp: Over the last couple of years we've used TV as our major medium supporting Anadin in a very competitive marketplace. But we were increasingly concerned at the rising cost of airtime and found we could not afford 2 or 3 bursts. That's not enough.

T.D.: I gather the press actually made you an offer.

Roy Bookman: In July 1984 Mirror Group Newspapers contacted us. They proposed a low cost press test in Scotland coupled with detailed research. It was too good an opportunity not to take up so we made the decision to take 40% of our TV spend and redeploy it in newspapers.

T.D.: What did the research show?

D.B.: As every marketing guy will tell you, TV works quickly while press has a slow burn effect. Interestingly though, at the end of the test, levels of awareness for both media were very similar. We were also looking at Anadin's unaided awareness level. At the start of the test, it stood at 45%, by the end, the level had risen by 18% which, for the analgesics market, is very significant. And particularly so when compared with other manufacturers who spent a lot more.

T.D.: How much was the press responsible?

R.B.: It had a great impact, fully justifying our decision to take money from TV. Firstly, we were able to afford a media presence of some forty weeks in the year using both media while our competitors who used TV as a solus medium tended to dip in and out. Secondly, our awareness increased dramatically while that of our rivals dropped.

T.D.: What actually happened to sales in Scotland?

D.B.: While 1985 was a very buoyant market, most of the traditional brands saw a decline in share. In Scotland, I'm pleased to say we bucked the trend and it became our second best sales area.

T.D.: What did you learn from the test?

R.B.: We learnt that mixed media works! We also wanted to see if we could replicate it successfully on a national basis and we are now doing just that . . .'

Radio

Radio is an increasingly important medium. Like television, it offers a wide variety of mass audiences which can be targeted through local radio stations.

Radio can be a dramatic and exciting way to present products, although there is the drawback that the products cannot be seen. This is a particularly important point if you are introducing a radically new product, but is not so important if you are presenting something 'invisible' such as a carrier service or a building society.

Like radio, television is a transient medium, and not suited for presenting complex products. But it does lend considerable prestige and can be extremely cheap.

In 1981 *The Daily Mail* ran a radio campaign for its classified pages, spending just £45,000, on two, four-week bursts on Capital Radio in London and Piccadilly Radio in Manchester. Over 200 30-second commercials ran on Capital alone for a dramatically successful campaign. The classified revenue increased by 22 per cent compared to the previous year, and despite a declining market. Also, market share increased at the expense of the *Mail's* two major competitors, *The Daily Telegraph* and *Daily Express*.

Posters

Posters are very much a mass audience medium, reaching everyone whenever they go out, having most impact on those groups who go out most, the young, the successful, and males.

More precise targeting can be achieved by careful siting. Posters on main roads and near petrol stations are obviously ideal for reaching motorists. Similarly, shopping areas are good for housewives, and off-licence sites well-placed for drinkers. However, it is difficult to reach a concentrated up-market audience because posters are usually excluded from high-class residential areas.

The first advantage of posters is sheer impact – they magnify the product being 'Big, bold and bloody', as they are commonly described. They can make even a small local advertiser look big in his particular area. Their sheer size may be an excellent way to familiarise people with new or changed products.

A poster's second advantage is repetition. Your audience may well be passing that poster at least twice a day, back and forth, on their way to work.

The disadvantage of posters is simplicity – usually you do not have room for more than a few words. Second, although posters may catch the passer-by, they usually do not get more than a passing glance. Finally, their cost is higher than any other medium, generally around 25 per cent of the space cost.

Direct marketing

Just as marketing is more than selling, so is direct marketing more than direct mail, or advertising that sells direct off-the-page. It comprises of three elements: direct mail; telemarketing; and door-to-door distribution and, if you like, off-the-page advertising.

Until recently, direct marketing was very much a second-class citizen within advertising, but that situation is changing. Direct marketing is the fastest expanding part of the advertising world. There is now hardly any major advertising agency that does not have a direct-marketing department or subsidiary, and many of these subsidiaries have only been bought up recently as advertising agencies have clamoured to get into this new fashionable area. David Ogilvy, founder of major advertising agency Ogilvy & Mather, has long insisted that 'one day all agencies will be direct-marketing agencies'. That day may not be so far away.

The major advantages of all forms of direct marketing is that they enable:

- Precise targeting of the market – they are a rifle compared to the shotgun of other forms of advertising.
- Precise costing – you know exactly what it costs to bring in so many sales.

Remember that precise targeting is the primary goal of all marketing. It may be fine for the ego as your television campaign is broadcast, but there are many instances where television will be far less effective and far more expensive than direct marketing.

The problem with all forms of direct marketing is that they have a poor image in the eyes of the public. One recent survey conducted by the Post Office showed that the public almost universally regard direct mail with great suspicion.

Direct mail

Direct mailing premits very precise targeting of prospects, thanks to ever more sophisticated computer files. Some companies are not yet aware of this. If they are selling an industrial product, for example, they will work on a scatter principle mailing all companies which they think might be interested, and all job titles that may be involved. In fact, with sophisticated market location lists which are available from a variety of agencies, it may be possible to find out the names of executives and their job titles in the companies concerned, who owns the companies, and even the cars driven by senior executives, with the result that considerable savings can be made on print and postage.

There are various lists of names that can be bought, a great many being all-purpose, available to all advertisers. There is a Nationwide Consumer File, for example, offering 40 million names at home addresses which can be broken down into family households; solus males and females; 17 to 21-year olds; with more information on high-status retirement areas with many single pensioners/married owner-occupiers/rented flats for the elderly/smart inner-city flats on company lets where there are very few children; post-1981 housing; council estates with middle-income small houses; high-status family enclaves in inner city areas, and so on. An added bonus is that all these lists are credit screened, which is extremely convenient for people such as retailers who want to mail the potential customers living close to their store.

You can also buy lists from companies which have created their own. A pram manufacturer, for example, may have built up a list of new customers from returned guarantee cards. All the mothers on that list will be excellent prospects for the manufacturers of baby foods. And the manufacturer may well be prepared to sell the list.

If you can, build your own database on customers, something that can now be done for less than a penny a head. Some of the key fields to put on such a database are:

Location: Where do customers live?
Demographic: What kind of people are they?
Psychographic: What motivates them?
Spending: How much do they spend?
Promotions: What promotions have you sent them?
Replies: What did they reply to and how?
Payments: Will they pay and how?
Timing: At what time of the year do they respond?

Databases can sometimes be built by clever promotions. Rothmans ran an in-pack promotion inviting the Rothmans' King Size smoker to return a draw ticket with his or her own name and address plus that of a draw partner – the prize was a pair of matched Opel Monza cars. The condition was that your draw partner should be an adult, a smoker, and a smoker of a brand other than Rothmans King Size. This was mailed to 500,000 Rothmans' King Size smokers, producing names and addresses for 250,000 smokers of competitive brands. Research showed that over 90 per cent were genuine.

Direct mail allows you to present products in great detail and, if you can afford it, in lavish colour brochures. Long brochures may well be essential if you are selling complex products and services such as insurance plans or holidays.

The disadvantage of direct mail is its negative associations and low prestige. Against this must be set the fact that many prestigious companies, including banks, financial services companies, American Express, political parties, charities and booksellers, do use direct mail.

Case History No 7. Direct mail: Royal Viking Line

This case is a good illustration of how direct mail can be used to target very small groups precisely and how, correctly used, it can sell prestigious products and services.

Royal Viking Line is the most expensive cruise line you can find offering luxury cruises to all parts of the world. Its target market is very small, very upmarket (earning £30,000 plus per annum) and thus difficult to reach economically through conventional media. So RVL committed its total advertising budget to direct marketing.

RVL's experience in the USA showed the period between prospect contact and conversion to be about two years. Research in the UK showed attitudes to cruising to be fairly negative, based on historical impressions of cruising as being for old people, and involving endless days at sea. So the task was to locate new prospects, and build the public's understanding of, and interest in modern cruising first.

Agency Ogilvy & Mather Direct used inserts in upmarket magazines and mailings to upmarket lists to locate potential customers (or prospects). Two key questions were asked: (1) Had they cruised before? and (2) With which line? All respondents were entered on a database.

Prospects were then segmented as separate targets and,

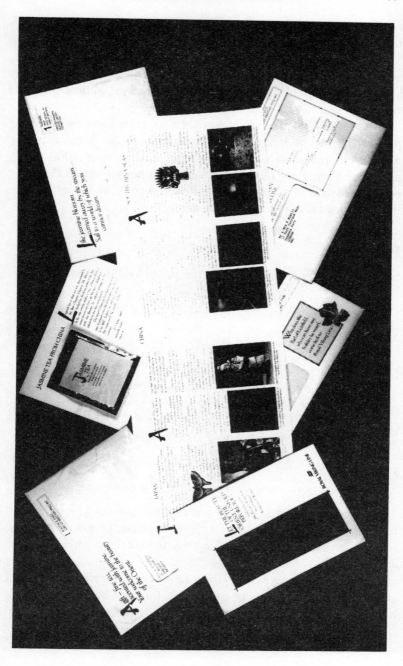

interestingly, mailed regularly six to eight times a year, to build up their interest in RVL. The range of destinations was used as an initial attraction, and backed up by RVL's special product benefits. Existing customers were also mailed regularly in a similar way – yielding a repeat booking rate of almost 50 per cent.

The results are that RVL has seen its sales increase by 400 per cent since it launched its campaign in the UK, and its number of passengers has risen from 250 to over 1000 plus paying an average of £5,000 per passenger per voyage. (OMDM rarely measure response to an individual pack as the effect of their mailings is cumulative over time.)

Example

Sample of direct mail letter from the Royal Viking Line

Mr A Sample

November 1986

Announcing new 1987 cruise programmes
Exciting new locations for you to visit . . .
to explore . . . our traditional
impeccable service. And this year . . .

Dear Mr Sample,

. . . some rather special incentives if you book early.

I thought I ought to write to you and send you our new brochure because this year we really have a most interesting programme – and some very good reasons for making this the year you cruise with us again.

I must confess our cruises have never been described as cheap. But then, if cheap holidays interested you, I doubt whether you would have inquired about Royal Viking Line in the first place.

However, this year, if you plan and book your cruise early, I have some rather special offers for you which will make your cruise not only memorable but also more *affordable*. But first let me tell you more about the coming year's programme.

You will find that once again we offer a wider range of *destinations* than any other cruise line, and a greater variety of *length of cruise*. You should find it easy to select a cruise that suits your taste and fits the time you have to spare. We have 68 cruises covering 6 continents across 22 areas. There are 140 ports of call with over 500 shore excursions to choose from.

Once again, we will not merely visit the well known sights, but also some refreshingly different ones. In particular, I think you will find our Leif Erikson itinerary – following the tracks of the legendary Viking explorer – and our cruises to China particularly appealing.

You may also find our cruise to Alaska a bracing, agreeable change from the usual sun-kissed climes. This cruise last year was outstandingly popular.

Which of your personal interests are we catering for this year?
Clients report that they do appreciate cruises that appeal to their personal interests. Accordingly, we have introduced more and more of these cruises.

For example: indulge your love of golf on our Jewels of the Orient cruise; your feeling for music on our Midnight Sun, Majestic Fjords cruise; and if you are a bridge fanatic I think you will find our South American cruise with Omar Sharif as guest player and teacher an exciting option.

Other celebrities you may encounter this year include Gary Player, Rixi Markus, Sir Yehudi Menuhin and Paul Tortelier.

As you would expect, we shall be striving once again to provide an even better service. There will be more staff to serve you than on other lines, more space for you te relax in, a greater variety of entertainment. And, perhaps more important, we are still dedicated to those little things that matter so much ... like remembering your name, cleaning your stateroom three times a day – in short doing everything to ensure our service matches anything you could expect even in the most splendid of hotels.

Please read on ....

A range of special incentives to tempt you.

If you book well in advance, you can ensure the choice of the best available stateroom.

Accordingly we are offering a 5% saving on any booking made before 31st January for any cruise departing after 1st April.

A little simple calculation will show you just how much that could save you on a cruise for two. In fact, when you consider that despite our higher levels of service and accommodation many of our prices overlap those of lines with a lower standard of service; this saving enables you to enjoy World Class cruising at less than the price of First Class on many ordinary cruises.

And there are many other incentives I would like to draw to your attention.

For instance, our air fares this year are very attractive. For the Alaska/Canada based cruises, only £149. For China and Japan, only £349. South America from as little as £329. And – best of all – air fares are FREE on Northern Europe – Baltic cruises: and this includes your return fare from New York if you take the Leif Erikson cruise.

If by any chance you are single, then we have a special offer, too. Normally, single accommodation is offered at a supplementary cost of 60%. But on five selected South American, Panama Canal and Bermuda-crossing cruises, the supplement is now only 25% extra.

Finally, if you decide to book two cruises in succession, we offer you a $250 saving on your booking. a splendid reason for doubling your pleasure this year.

Once again, your chauffeur-driven car awaits.

If you are either embarking or disembarking at Southampton, we offer you a complimentary chauffer-driven car from your home if it's in London or Home Counties, or from either London airport. A most relaxing prelude to your cruise. And, once again, we have arranged some cruises at very modest prices – starting as low as £1,457 – even less if you take advantage of our saving.

I know many people enjoy looking through our brochure and contemplating the delights we have in store. I hope you will find this particular edition a pleasure to browse through . . . and even more, that it whets your appetite for the cruises we have planned for you this year.

Booking is very simple. Just go to your nearest travel agent who will handle matters for you. If you have any questions – or you would like us to recommend an agent to you – call us on 01-734 0773/4/5.

You will also see enclosed with this letter is a little Questionnaire – I would appreciate it if you could spare the time to return it to us, because it enables us to offer a better service to our clients.

Yours sincerely,

P.S. Last year more people than ever befoe decided to enjoy a Royal Viking Line cruise. Sadly, some who left their booking late had to be disappointed – either they could not get the staterooms they had preferred or even had to settle for cruises other than the one they particularly wanted. Consequently, if you do have a particular cruise in mind, *please don't delay*. Get in touch with us and we'll ensure you get what you want (as well as your 5% saving).

Telemarketing

Telemarketing is a form of promotion that is still largely ignored in the UK, but in the USA the telephone is the largest single direct response medium with an expenditure estimated at $37.5 billion, way ahead of television, press or mail. The telephone is ideal in many respects. It not only enables you to reach customers directly, but allows them to tell you what *they* think. That means you can learn quickly and adapt your message, which is impossible with a direct-mail message as 100,000 copies are passing through the Post Office. In addition, telemarketing is measurable and relatively cheap and easy – you do not have to make a massive investment in production, artwork, photography or print.

A good example of how flexible telemarketing can be, comes from the experience of TMS, British Telecom's own Telephone Marketing Service. It was employed by a Dutch book club to telephone lapsed members with a special offer designed to bring them back into the fold. TMS operators did some research to discover why old customers had lost interest. It emerged that the main reason was that people felt they probably had enough books at home already. So, TMS persuaded the club to replace the typical special offer of free books, or so many books at a low price, with a non-book offer. The result – TMS boosted the renewal rate from 3 per cent to 22 per cent overnight.

Costs can vary however. One successful telemarketing agency calculates that to set up a telemarketing exercise will cost between £750 and £4,000, depending on the extent of briefing, the complexity of the script used, and the cost of creating a handbook to be used by telemarketers to handle objections. Then there is the cost of the actual calls which is normally in the region of £4 per contact. The agency advises clients to run an initial test of up to 1,000 calls before undertaking the full programme.

The telephone has the disadvantage that the product cannot be seen, and it does not lend itself naturally to detailed product descriptions. But it does have that all-important element of personal contact.

Certainly there is a question of ethics hanging over this medium. The telephone is a high-pressure sales instrument which has to be treated with discretion. It can also be damaging to sellers because many people will say 'yes' merely to end a phone conversation, with the result that the representative finds himself sitting on a pile of useless leads. Finally, when considering telemarketing do not ignore the fact that it can help build up a database for direct mail campaigns.

Door-to-door distribution

This is another fast growing area of direct marketing, especially since the launch of a new centralised Royal Mail Household Delivery Service at the beginning of 1987. In 1985 and 1986 this service distributed about 700 million items, handling the AIDS leaflets delivered to all 23 million addresses in the UK.

Such door-to-door distribution is normally targeted by post codes or television area, and can include unaddressed mail. Booking can be extremely rapid and is normally within 24 hours and certainly within 48 hours.

Door-to-door is essentially another form of direct mail, and needs little more to be said about it than that it is a very useful form of targeting a particular area and is ideal for local stores.

6
Planning Public Relations

Public relations

Public relations (PR) has, for many people, sinister associations of brainwashing. This is partly because they are confused about just what PR people do, and admittedly it is very difficult to sum up PR because so many activities are involved.

Basically PR involves communicating with all those associated with an organisation, which might include staff, sales force, shareholders, local communities, relevant authorities and government departments, as well as the general public.

There are two kinds of communication – direct and indirect. Indirect communication is usually more important, with the PR people supplying the media with information in various forms in order to gain their unbiased coverage. If successful they will gain press coverage through a variety of methods, including press releases, press receptions, personal contacts with journalists, feature articles, supply of technical data and information, photographs, and so on.

- *Television coverage* – through similar methods, including news releases and conferences, documentary films and videos.
- *Radio coverage* – again through similar methods, and the supply of tapes.

There are other methods by which PR agencies attract media attention, notably:

- Stunts, such as the pop group sending off famous groups' recordings under its own name, and getting no play.

- Events, such as competitions like the Styrofoam Raft Race, wine tastings, fashion shows, and so on.
- Sponsorships – attaching the client's name to such events as races, shows, expeditions, feats and exhibitions.

PR may also involve direct communication with the general public, staff and others via:

- Conferences, seminars and shows.
- Publicity literature and educational material.
- House journals, and so on.

In-house PR will be particularly important for a large organisation determined to boost morale among its employees, particularly large official organisations such as government departments, the police and health institutions. In-house PR will also be important for a financial organisation which wants to inform intermediaries and brokers about its latest products and services, or a car manufacturer with similar goals vis-à-vis dealers.

The first great advantage of PR is cost. Advertising, it is said, costs money – money for space, airtime and the production of the advertisement. But PR only costs the time of the consultants involved, although that can add up too. The result can be publicity worth a fortune, costing a pittance. Publishers, for example, have puny budgets, yet by arranging press and television interviews for authors can achieve coverage worth millions in terms of sheer space.

The second great advantage of PR is credibility, precisely because its end result is impartial coverage of the product by the media. It is an ideal supplement to advertising as well as, in extremis, a replacement.

When Wiggins Teape, a major British paper manufacturer, launched Courier, a new range of office paper, it used a multi-channel campaign, embracing trade press advertising, sales promotion and a PR package. There was also a press conference adapted from a series of highly dramatic sales meetings, press interviews and newsletters involving independent sales forces in the distribution chain. It would not have been practical to try and address all Wiggins Teape's various publics – suppliers, users, buyers, secretaries and sales force – through a single advertising campaign.

PR may be essential when you are promoting a complex or a new product, and all the product benefits and features cannot be included in the advertising. For example, if you are selling a new car you will naturally want it featured in the motoring sections of the press. Similarly, if you are promoting any technical product, it will be important to get write-ups in technical journals.

An extraordinary range of products and services can benefit from PR, even fast-moving consumer goods. Shredded Wheat is an interesting example of a total communications campaign. It had long been marketed as a natural, satisfying breakfast cereal. Then the new health consciousness of the 1980s led to a complete rethink of its positioning. Here, Nabisco realised, was a complete health food, high in fibre, low in fat, with no added sugar or salt.

A relaunch campaign was developed, involving humorous yet informative advertising on the 'Mr Perky' theme, new packaging, health-oriented promotions, internal company communications and brand publicity.

An extensive PR campaign involved another excellent device, the establishment of the Shredded Wheat Fibre Information Centre. This in turn published a booklet *Healthy Eating,* endorsed by the Health Education Council. It also made extensive contacts with various professionals, including nutritionists, dietitians and health visitors, who all testified to the product's health values. Since that 1985 relaunch, sales have grown by 20 per cent, no mean achievement for such an established brand.

Many of the PR person's functions, such as providing press releases, are fairly routine. But considerable imagination is called for in creating 'stunts' and other attention-grabbing events. There are stand-bys, though. One is the survey. If a school fees planning service, for example, wants to draw attention to itself, it can conduct a survey which shows that, say, 80 per cent of parents paying for their children's education have to make considerable sacrifices. That may merit a mention in the press and radio.

Sponsorships are a much debated form of PR, but there is no doubt they can work. Daihatsu was not a very well-known name among Japanese companies. Yet as a result of sponsoring the Bob Hope Classic in 1980 it received many new orders for its golf cart and other Daihatsu vehicles, in the three weeks following the golf championship. George Griffith, director of sales, could be certain of this because the golf cart was not being promoted in any way at the time of the tournament. Even if sponsorships can only communicate a name, that in itself may be enough.

Case History No 8. Public Relations: The Styrofoam Raft Race

The product was Styrofoam board, a building insulation material. The problem was how to boost awareness among architects. Burson-Marsteller took on the problem in 1984, agreeing targets for the Styrofoam messages of 88 per cent coverage of architects with the result of 6.5 'opportunities to see' (OTS).

They came up with a simple and ingenious idea – a national raft race for architects – to show just how much PR can achieve. Each competing practice would receive free Styrofoam with which to build a raft. The rationale was that this would not only boost brand awareness, but provide hands-on experience of its USPs (water resistance and mechanical strength), and yield sales leads.

Five heats were arranged leading to national finals at Henley. During the heats, pre-publicity, press attendance and picture story follow-ups secured extensive coverage on local radio and in daily/weekly local newspapers. An eve-of-event London preview obtained advance coverage for the finals on regional television including Thames News, and in *The Times*, *The Daily Telegraph* and *The Guardian*. The final was recorded by the BBC and shown on the early evening news. Film coverage showed the

camera closing in on the product name, which was also mentioned in the commentary. Other television regions, including Thames, also covered the event along with over 40 regional, daily and local weekly papers.

By every criterion the raft race was a success. Later promotional analysis showed that the event had scored 90 per cent coverage for Styrofoam, with 6.9 OTS among architects. Between 150 and 200 architects came into direct contact with Styrofoam as a result of the event, and informal research showed they had acquired a considerable appreciation of the product's USP.

One important function of PR may be defensive, such as handling a crisis. When the DHSS found an abnormal number of salmonella cases in babies fed on Ostermilks, Farley reacted quickly withdrawing the product on 20 December 1985, and mounted a big PR education campaign. All major customers were called immediately and arrangements made to pick up the product. Health visitors received a direct mailing from the company. A programme was set up for consumers to return Ostermilks purchased, and received other products in exchange. Also, a media centre was set up to handle enquiries and update information as and when received.

Traces of salmonella had been first discovered at Farley's Kendal plant on 3 December. Statements were immediately made to the press, and a clean-up of the factory begun. The Farley salesforce was thoroughly trained to answer questions and explain to the public and media exactly what the situation was, halting speculation. The results of this prompt and extensive campaign became clear later when the company was sold for a very satisfactory price. The only real asset of the company was its goodwill, since its products had been off the shelves for six months.

Summary: The Media Mix

Having considered all possible means of reaching your market, you are now in a position to decide on the main part of your marketing plan, the media mix.

How you apportion your total promotional budget between different media will depend to a great extent on how you have defined your target market and broken it down into segments. Your aim should be to achieve the maximum coverage with maximum impact and comprehensibility at minimum cost.

This is where experienced media planners can be of great use. They can produce intricate models, accurately calculating the total audiences, with total OTS and other relevant factors produced by different outlays.

Whatever you decide, you should have a clear plan precisely setting out your target audiences and expenditure for each medium. You should also define in advance how you are going to quantify results in such terms as the number of new users of the product, increase in brand awareness, coupon response rate, and whatever other criteria may apply to your particular situation.

General principles are that it is better to concentrate on one medium and one particular form of that medium – one newspaper, for example – for maximum impact. Similarly, it is better to publish a small number of large advertisements than many small ones. And it is better to reach a small part of the total potential market strongly than all of it with a feeble message.

The big spending advertisers seem to follow these principles in committing most of their money to television. But remember that the automatic choice, such as television, may not be the best medium for your product. A media mix may be essential to put across the product's virtues. Television may be useful to draw attention to a new insurance product, for example, but press and/or brochures may be essential to explain it in detail. A PR programme may be invaluable if you have a good product story to tell, such as the Shredded Wheat example (page 87) and can influence authorities and opinion-makers as well as the general public.

The different media can also complement each other in terms of timing. Sales promotions, which we shall come to, and PR can help boost sales at times when they are normally stagnant, so it is not worth spending on more expensive media.

One medium can often complete the sales initiated by another. Direct mail or door-to-door distributions will probably be vastly more effective on the back of a television or press campaign, and telemarketing can convert wavering potential customers after a direct mailing. Cost should not be the be-all and end-all in forming your overall plan. The cheapest medium may not be the best in terms of its powers of presentation or prestige.

A general principle is to build flexibility into your plan. Most promotions will, to some extent, be trips into the unknown. Allow yourself as much room as possible to change the plan if it does not work out. Experiment on a small scale first if it is possible.

Finally, put your plan into action, and wait anxiously to see if all the theorising and rationalising has paid off!

7
Planning Sales Promotion and Merchandising

Sales promotion

Sales promotion is an increasingly powerful weapon in the marketing manager's armoury. Broadly defined, it enhances the sales of selected goods and services by the application of more or less subtle bribery, or making 'offers'.

By offering added *tangible* (rather than perceived) benefit to a product – such as money off the purchase – it may also serve to reinforce product branding in the consumer's mind. For this reason, sales promotion is frequently used in harness with advertising – which is mainly concerned with image and positioning – when launching or promoting a product.

Merchandising is often confused with sales promotion, of which it is only a part. Merchandising is the deployment of certain sales promotion techniques (sometimes including *tactical*, as opposed to brand advertising) which are essentially short-term in their objectives.

Its origins are in the travelling pedlar or market-stall holder who encouraged sales of his wares by allowing customers to 'feel the goods'. Merchandising plays on the powerful psychological truth that if customers become involved with the product, they are much more likely to buy it.

Sales promotion, however, has an increasingly strategic element in its implementation. A number of specialist consultancies have sprung up – such as KLP, FKB, IMP and Marketing Solutions – which give advice on long-term problem solving. Like advertising agencies, which they increasingly resemble (and to which they are often allied), sales promotion consultancies talk of their work as a 'campaign' or 'marketing strategy'. In fact, sales promotion (including merchandising) is increasingly usurping the functions of both the company sales force and the advertising agency. Some of the reasons are as follows:

- The high cost of labour, and the deteriorating quality of staff in retail distribution, has meant that personal salesmanship is disappearing from the High Street. The more impersonal environment of supermarkets and multiple stores has meant that merchandising now plays a much more important role in enabling products to 'speak for themselves'.
- The high cost of the major media – television and the press – has made many advertisers look for cheaper ways of promoting their brands. The trend away from advertising and towards what are called consumer promotions has been particularly marked in the USA over the past 10 years and is beginning to make an impact in the UK. But the danger in switching money away from advertising is that in the long run it tends to undermine the branding of a product.
- Partly because of the above, the market application of sales promotion has broadened remarkably in the past few years. Originally it was restricted to FMCG goods. It was overwhelming groceries in the supermarket, there was some point-of-sale (POS) activity in pubs and off-licences (for example on beer mats, founts and display stands) and on the garage forecourt.

Now everyone is in on the act, and one of the biggest converts has been financial services. A good example can be seen in the way banks and building societies are competing for funds in the High Street by offering special high interest, or incentivised accounts.

The credit card and charge-card companies have been particularly active in the field. In 1985, for example, KLP introduced a dividend scheme for Diners which offered customers valuable gifts on a points system related to the number of purchases made. The aim was to get customers to use their Diners in preference to other plastic cards. Imitation being the sincerest form of flattery, Barclaycard has now adopted a similar scheme called Profiles.

Another enthusiastic user of sales promotions has been the Government. Last year the Department of Energy ran a 'Monergy' campaign, designed to help consumers cut down their fuel bills. The campaign incidentally showed how national advertising (in this case Saatchi and Saatchi) is being increasingly linked to sales promotion (handled by FKB), and indeed the strategic role played by sales promotion consultancies.

The advertisements invited consumers to ring in, using a freephone, to find out how to economise on energy. The sales promotion/consultancy tracked the enquiries, sent out energy-saving information packs and at the same time built up a comprehensive database for the department's future use.

In fact sales promotion rarely works in isolation from other forms of advertising. It has clear affinities with direct marketing (for example, mail shots), but also design (particularly packaging) in the sense that displays and packs can provide important support for a product at the point-of-sale (ie on the shelves).

Point-of-sale (POS)

A recent survey by the Market Research Society disclosed that 20 per cent of all purchasing decisions are made by housewives in the shop – a telling point about the importance of getting merchandising right in-store. There are several golden rules or at least aspects of POS psychology to be mastered.

One is to create a good layout for the stands holding your product. This means not only creating something eye-catching for the consumer, but a practical design which stands up properly and holds the products it is designed to take. One product well displayed is often worth 50 mounted as a spectacular pyramid, which no one will touch for fear of upsetting the display. You should also bear in mind that a good layout is of as much value to the retailer as the customer. Ideally the stand should make it crystal clear to him when your brand needs restocking *before* it ceases to become available to the consumer. Another trick is to help the consumer remember the advertising support (and the branding). This may be done by reiterating the company or product logo, or using a consistent merchandising shape which reminds people of what they have seen on the advertisements.

Perhaps the best-known aspect of POS psychology is the importance of placing products at eye level, or next to the cash register wherever possible. Research carried out mainly in the USA, but backed up in the UK, suggests that up to 60 per cent increase in sales results from moving the product from ground to eye level. The logic behind this seemingly obvious point is that in many mass markets consumers are faced with a bewildering variety of brands of more or less equivalent appeal. The brand they first see has a much better chance of being sold.

Types of promotion

As suggested above, sales promotion is not merely concerned with the consumer, but also serves to motivate the retailer, the distributer who has to sell to the retailer, and indeed your company's sales force itself.

An interesting example of sales-force motivation is supplied by Sketchley, the High Street dry cleaners. As market leader it was forbidden to expand in an already stagnant market by the Monopolies and Mergers Commission. In order to grow it had to increase revenue per customer through additional services, which meant motivating the staff to make the public aware of them.

Option One, the sales promotion consultancy used by Sketchley, got around this problem by hiring 'mystery shoppers' who handed a five pound note as a prize to staff who offered them the new services. There was also a branch draw to increase team morale. Option One subsequently claimed sales of the extra services increased 600 per cent during the period of the promotion, and continued at 300 per cent for some time afterwards.

On occasions, incentive schemes may be applicable to all

three areas of salesforce, distributor and customer. Here is an example from the holiday market concerning Swan National Incentive Breaks.

Car rentals tend to fall away dramatically at the weekend. In 1984 Swan National began to address this problem by offering customers a weekends-away package, which included two nights' accommodation in more than 300 hotels and guest houses, breakfast, a choice of car from the company fleet with unlimited mileage, and built-in service charges and VAT.

It proved so successful that the following year Swan diversified into the business incentive market. Argyll Group and Beefeater Steak Houses, for example, used the scheme for part of a customer-incentive promotion. Britvic used a version as a joint customer offering dealer incentives in 10,000 pubs. And Bosch (motor division) ran a dealer promotion in 36,000 outlets offering five 'Weekends Away' worth £500 each.

Merchandising techniques

As said earlier, merchandising is the part of sales promotion tangibly concerned with generating consumer interest in a product or service. Some of the commonest examples of the techniques involved are set out below, with examples of how they may be employed.

- The Self-Liquidating Premium offer (SLP). This amounts to giving away at cost price items such as garden shears, prints or coffee tables in return for proof of purchase, such as packet tops. Money is sometimes substituted for the gift. The SLP is an old favourite with partwork magazines (magazines to be collected, the complete set forming an encyclopedia), and is useful in stimulating interest demand for later magazines in the series once the initial burst of (highly expensive) television advertising begins to wear off.
- Free gifts are a related area, aimed at stimulating impulse purchases (for example a free toothbrush with every large tube of toothpaste; a free fluorescent bracelet with a girl's

comic). The *mail-in* is a variant where the gift, usually intrinsically more valuable than the above, can only be claimed by sending in a number of tokens or packet tops from the promoted product. The mail-in is a favourite with breakfast cereal companies such as Kelloggs and Quaker Oats.

A more complex example is provided by Pickford Travel, which was seeking to persuade people that there was plenty of scope for late booking package holidays. Option One, the sales promotion consultancy handling the account, hit upon the idea of using a personality, Henry Cooper, with the slogan 'Don't throw in the towel!' The premium gift was a free beach towel with every booking. In this instance there was no possibility of back-of-the pack information and proof of purchase, as with grocery items. Instead, promotion was carried out through leaflets and direct mail. Pickfords, which had aimed to sell 6,000 extra bookings, actually sold 8,000.

- Cash premium and money-off vouchers are much loved. The vouchers may be distributed in a variety of ways, through the letter box, printed on the back of packs to encourage repeat purchases, or published in magazines and newspapers. Although highly effective when properly used, the voucher method can backfire through what is called *malredemption*, which generally occurs when the retailer (in many areas these days an all-powerful force) takes it upon himself to accept coupons indiscriminately for products related to the one being promoted. This effectively forces the manufacturer to subsidise his rivals.
- Games and competitions are a very powerful promotional device. When used properly they have a strong addictive appeal. Scratchcard garage forecourt promotions – where consumers are invited to match up different symbols and walk off with a large cash prize (when they get the right card) – recently enjoyed an enthusiastic revival among the major petrol companies. But these competitions are very expensive to run, as they entail substantial television and press

advertising to stimulate consumer interest. But in the stagnant petrol retail market, it proved a good deal cheaper than price discounting.

Fleet Street, which is constantly battling to improve circulation figures, has taken a similar route with the bingo-type competition. *The Times* initially added considerably to its sales with a stocks-and-shares game called Portfolio. But the gains are generally short-term. Great care has to be taken to achieve actuarial accuracy with these competitions to guarantee a manageable number of winners (otherwise the competition becomes an uneconomic burden on the advertiser).

Other methods of merchandising include free samples (getting the consumer to use the product) and bargain packs, where the manufacturer offers extra product for the normal retail price.

Trade merchandising

Techniques for selling to the retailer (and dominating substantial shelf space) are numerous. They include the baker's dozen principle, where the dealer/retailer is offered extra product and percentage discounts for bulk orders. In some cases there is a cash incentive linked to the amount of product which the dealer manages to shift.

One variant is the cooperative advertising scheme, in which the manufacturer/supplier puts up part of the dealer's advertising budget or includes the dealer's name in national or local advertising.

8
Exhibitions, Conferences and Seminars

The unique virtue of exhibitions, conferences and seminars is that customers actually seek out the producer, and often tell him exactly what they need. As a result, sales leads can be created at a cost far below that of advertising or direct sales canvassing, and the rate of conversion can be much higher.

Another distinctive feature of exhibitions, seminars and conferences is that they are all ideal for demonstrating products and services, particularly those which are difficult to describe or need to be seen in action, or touched. A classic example is the fruit juice extractor variety of product sometimes shown at the Ideal Home Exhibition.

All of these events provide an intimate, personal environment. Even a Wembley Centre can have a very emotional effect, as Sir Michael Edwardes found when he asked for far-ranging measures of support from his Leyland dealers, and received a standing ovation.

Each medium is suitable for different types of audience. Exhibitions deal generally with unknown customers, conferences with large numbers of known salespeople and staff, while seminars may also deal with staff but are more intimate and interactive.

Exhibitions

Exhibitions can sometimes be fun and sometimes very tiresome. The decision whether to attend one, or for that matter create a conference or seminar programme, requires careful considera-tion and an explicit statement of objectives. They should be planned annually in advance, answering two points:

1. What is the annual budget and what type of exhibitions will be attended?
2. Which products out of a range should be exhibited? If all are shown, will it have too fragmented an effect?

Then you can go on to set more detailed objectives by asking the following questions:

3. What is to be achieved by attending exhibitions? They can be used to meet potential new clients and reinforce existing relationships; provide a platform for the launch of new products, demonstrate the product to potential customers, act as a focus to link with new agents and dealers and, finally, give the opportunity of matching and meeting competitors' efforts. Which are your objectives?
4. How will you assess whether you have been successful? Auditing exhibition success is extremely difficult, but attempts must be made. It is possible to calculate the cost per visitor reached (someone who has stopped to talk or acquire literature, was interested in the product and remembers visiting the stand). Regardless of the type of exhibition, the average cost of a visitor reached in 1986 was £423; in 1985 £424; and in 1984 £421. These figures increase by about 20 per cent when fully loaded with salesmen's expenses, and so on, and compare extremely well with personal selling.
5. Are exhibition decisions rooted in reality? Are the expectations too high, budgets too low and resources too thin? Never undertake to have an exhibition stand 'on the cheap'.
6. Is there any information on competitors' performance at the exhibition? Again the exhibition organiser should be able to help. Although not foolproof, a rebooking of a stand – particularly of a larger size – would indicate a satisfactory performance.

Without such clear objectives exhibitions can be a terrible drain on resources. Prestigious stands costing designer budgets, developed to satisfy the managing director's ego and colour coordinated by his wife do not usually work.

When deciding which exhibitions to attend, prime emphasis should be given to who will be attending. For instance, vendors of vintage port might find it more cost-effective to exhibit at swimming pool, boat and Horse of the Year shows than at a specific wine exhibition. Lists of exhibitions are found in trade journals and the *Exhibition Bulletin*, which gives details of UK and international exhibitions.

Before you select an exhibition, check the exhibition organiser's claims about who is likely to visit the show. Previous visitors' lists will help. Also remember that, on average, only 10 to 20 per cent of exhibition visitors will call at any one stand. Check whether lists of visitors will be available after the exhibition. Research shows that, regardless of the type of exhibition, each visitor will only visit 13 stands. So the value of a list for direct canvassing is huge and, if it cannot be provided through an analysis of registration, express your concern. Do not select an exhibition solely by the profile of other exhibitors. They might have quite different aims and objectives.

Conferences

Conferences can be a very valuable promotional tool. They satisfy definite social needs, encourage group identity and corporate spirit, and provide a forum for the exchange of information, generally in three broad areas:

1. *Product launches.* A well-organised product launch can capture the imagination of the sales team, and even the public at large.
2. *Sales.* The sales conference provides ideal learning opportunities, not only within the formal sessions but also, and just as importantly, in the informal discussions which take place over lunch or in the bar where delegates can learn from each other.
3. *Incentive rewards.* Motor manufacturers, computer firms and life assurance companies build the exotic conference venue into their standard sales motivation and incentive programme. It is not unknown for a life assurance company to spend well over £500,000 on such an event.

There are many examples of successful conferences which meet these objectives. There was the essentially informational conference held by the Prudential to introduce its new corporate image 'Prudence'; there are new product launch conferences, as held by Ford to promote a new model; there are inspirational conferences, such as the evangelist meetings of Billy Graham; there are motivational conferences, such as the occasional week in the Virgin Islands to discuss corporate objectives and sales targets in more attractive surroundings, sometimes as part of an incentive award scheme. (Care has to be taken that any personal tax implications for delegates attending such conferences are discussed with the Inland Revenue in advance.)

Planning is always the key to a successful event. An over-long conference is expensive in both cash terms and in the cost penalty of lost opportunities for those attending who are away from their usual work. Meetings of this type are highly visible events, and getting it right can bring benefits far beyond the successful achievement of the stated objectives. Getting it wrong, however, can have repercussions from which it may take months to recover.

Case History No 9. Conferences: International Apple University Consortium

The 1986 conference organised by Apple, the personal computer company, illustrates perfectly the various uses of conferences. The main goal was to show how effective the Apple Macintosh computer is in education, and a conference provided a natural setting for exploring such a rich and complex product.

The Apple University Consortium was formed in 1984. Two years later the UK was host country for its first international event. In addition to demonstrating the Macintosh, the conference provided an opportunity to create a unique forum for the exchange of ideas, a forum also unique in being tailored to meet the needs of a wide and disparate international audience consisting of academics, professionals, the media, key opinion formers and all members of the AUC.

Cambridge University, being one of the oldest seats of learning, was chosen as a natural location. A strong relationship had already been built between Apple and the university's computer science department. The conference was meticulously organised. It had a design and theme – The Wheels for the Mind – running through the conference set, and all documentation and merchandise, such as conference bags. There were various speakers, and a 3-day exhibition display for which over 30 companies supplied software. There was even entertainment including a medieval banquet.

Alongside the conference there was pre- and post-conference publicity, with an on-site press office manned 24-hours-a-day. Interviews were arranged with key Apple executives. An exclusive interview with *Chief Executive* magazine resulted in Apple supremo, John Sculley, gaining front-page coverage.

The conference was a great success. Over 400 delegates from 38 different countries attended – far more than anticipated – including many key UK and international opinion formers. Many new international university relationships were formed. Apple was clearly positioned in the field of education as an innovator in information technology and gained extensive UK and international media coverage.

Seminars

Seminars can be one of the most powerful ways of forging a united, committed group of people, whether it be a group of customers committed to buying a product, or a group of managers and salesmen committed to producing and selling it. The power of seminars, of course, depends to a great extent on the expertise of the presenter and the peer group atmosphere among the audience.

Seminars have the advantage that they can be tailored precisely to different audiences, and taken to any place for any group. They can be varied in content to reflect the specific interests of audiences, and can be interactive – ideal for putting across detailed, complicated ideas.

Seminar selling can therefore be one of the most efficient uses of a sales representative's time, and has been practised to perfection by organisations such as Tupperware, selling kitchen goods to women in their own homes. The seminar has grown to be used for sales training, new product launches, company briefings and problem-solving exercises, because of the opportunities for two-way communication.

9
Pricing

For all the expertise devoted to other elements in the process of successfully marketing a product or service, pricing plays a unique role. It is the source of revenue which leads to profit, whereas all the other activities involve cost. For that reason alone, pricing is the jewel in the marketing manager's crown.

The harsh reality of this statement is enshrined in a comment overheard at a dinner party with a group of American bankers: 'There ain't no brand loyalty that two cents off can't overcome.' A little extreme perhaps, but, depending on the market for the product, it acts as a salutary reminder for those who would rush headlong into an expensive promotional campaign to increase market share.

Given this focus on the significance of pricing it cannot be considered in isolation: any profitable organisation must consider its place in the overall marketing mix when examining its profit objectives. Just to orientate the price of the product to costs fails to take into account the importance of demand, customer psychology and competitor behaviour.

There are four circumstances when decisions relating to price need to be considered:

1. In setting the price for a product for the first time. This occurs when entering a new market or offering a new product, or when bidding for a new contract.
2. When initiating a price change – either downwards to reflect cost savings, or upwards to cover increased costs or more profitable opportunities.
3. When the competition initiates a price change leading to the need for wider-ranging decisions to be made. Should you

respond with a price rise, or maintain price and challenge the competitor, or change markets completely?

4. When launching a product new to you but not the public, care is needed to keep internal consistency so as not to interfere with the profitability of the range, thus securing incremental, and not substitute revenues.

Under any of these circumstances, the two overriding considerations must be to ensure that first your pricing strategy fits the overall objectives of the business and, second, fits the positioning of the business and its products.

Is the company going for profits, increased revenues, or to expand and stake a claim to a certain size market share? For example, if the product is unique and a market can be defined which is prepared to pay almost anything for it, then a market skimming approach can be employed. In this instance the highest price possible is selected to provide high profits for as long as the consumer and the competition allow (this is often referred to as 'premier pricing').

Careful management of the process does allow revision, usually pushing the price down and opening the product to a wider selection of the whole market (economists refer to the price becoming 'more elastic'). This approach is commonly used in niche marketing and is typical of status goods such as colour televisions, videos and personal computers. However, the consumer is now very alert to such strategies and will readily wait for the 'mass market price', so be warned.

Increased revenue pricing usually applies where an early cash recovery is important, or the instability of the market is too great to justify long-term development. Children's fad toys and some marketing text books are two such examples.

Finally, market share pricing is designed to create a foothold in a market, or to expand an exisiting position to become preeminent and make the entry into the market prohibitively expensive for any competitors. The destruction of the British motor cycle industry by the Japanese is an obvious and painful example of this 'sell at any price' mentality. A tactical variation of this approach is promotional or loss-leader pricing. Life assurance companies will offer extremely attractive terms on one contract to attract a consumer, and cross-sell him with more profitable contracts.

In market share pricing, once ownership is achieved and price control is firmly within the company's grasp, high profits can be attained. These tactics are not restricted to multinational, pan–European markets. They apply equally well to the pricing of haircuts in the local High Street, as they do to the price of oil set by OPEC.

Pricing can also be a very important part of positioning a product. High prices may, in the consumer's eyes, reflect high-quality products, and low prices low quality. And people naturally come to associate a certain range of prices with a certain producer. We have different price expectations when shopping in Harrods, Marks and Spencer, and Woolworth, so care has to be taken to make the price fit both an individual product and a product range. In certain cases, for example, too low prices can even lead to reduced sales! Some producers of computer software have found that pricing their packages much lower than established market leaders has evoked 'cheap and nasty' associations (often undeserved), repelling rather than attracting customers.

Once the marketing (including pricing) objectives are defined, the task of fixing the price should be undertaken. Again, there are a number of places to start this process. One option is to calculate the production costs of the product and simply add to, or mark up, that price to reflect the return on investment required. This is a favourite mechanism used by most retailers when marking up the manufactured goods they sell by their own profit margins. A more complicated option is to try to anticipate the demand for the product, based upon the consumer's perception of the value of the product and its price. Take, for instance, legal fees: while they are usually viewed as being too high, the demand for a lawyer's perceived skills maintains a buoyant price.

This 'demand-orientated' pricing approach requires a more integrated marketing overview, which needs considerable knowledge of the target market for the product. It also requires an indication of the perceived quality of the product. In order to evaluate this, and how it should be reflected in the actual price charged, special market research techniques have been developed. Two of these methods involve 'rating' the price, either against absolutes (eg what price would the consumer pay for this product against a rival offer – this is used where the product is familiar, such as a new light switch), or comparatively against products in the same market. Here, for instance, a new electrical appliance would be judged by positioning it against the price of a kettle and a blender. If it was perceived to have more value than the kettle but less than a blender, the pricing range of this new appliance would be defined. Provided this produced an acceptable profit, the price is fixed.

A derivation of demand-orientated pricing is differential pricing. This requires even greater knowledge of the perceived value of the product within the target market. It also requires that the markets into which the differentially priced product is sold are discrete. This is essential because if the lower-priced product could be sold at a higher price then not only would revenue be lost, but so would the ability to control the price – it would be self-defeating.

Differential pricing is determined in one of four ways:

1. *Customer bias* – continental holidays, where families with children at school pay a premium to take their vacation in the school holidays, or where the need to be secure in the resort chosen is important.

2. *Product variations* – where the standard model is changed only slightly to distinguish it, and is then sold at a price higher than the marginal costs of the change.

3. *Place variation* – where the venue of purchase changes the price in excess of the additional cost of distribution. Anyone who has bought a pint of beer in a five-star hotel and then compares that with his local pub will understand!

4. *Time bias* – where the time at which the purchase is made determines the incremental cost of the product. Coal is a prime example. It goes down in price in the summer, and increases in winter when demand is immediate.

The final pricing process is to take account of the competition. By fixing the price with reference to the competition, the selected price is likely to be in the right region, but this 'going rate' basis has its faults. What if no comparable product exists? What is the cost of production to the competitor? Do they have a competitive edge? Answers to these questions can prove very difficult. This approach, however, is less likely to cause difficulties if the product is a service – for example, accountancy – as capital is not locked up in expensive fixed assets.

As with most things, the easiest procedures to implement – the mark-up and the going rate – are not the most profit efficient. What they gain in simplicity they lose in flexibility to maximise profit. Maximum profit requires awareness of demand. And demand-orientated examples allow for consumer desire and give more options to secure high profits.

The last pricing circumstance to be considered is initiating price changes. This can involve leading the market up or down, or be a response to competitors' moves. The domestic mortgage rate is a typical example where preeminent players in the market can force it to change.

Price changes are caused by consumer demand, or lack of it, by competitive pressures (as was the case with the 1986/7 fight between the new and established London evening newspapers), or by changing the costs of production. The ease with which movement can be achieved ultimately depends upon the market demand for the products. Where cheap substitutes exist, movement upward might be severely restricted, whereas in an almost monopolistic market practically any price can be charged. This certainly seems to be the case with credit card issuers Visa and Mastercard, which are currently being investigated by the Monopolies Commission.

In conclusion, in spite of the increased use of other factors in the marketing mix, price is an important element, and successfully fixing a price is especially challenging for new products. Attention must be paid to the pricing objective, policies and procedures. But above all, good knowledge of the costs of production and selling, understanding of consumer demand and an awareness of the competitors' likely reactions determine how successful the chosen price will be.

Everything has its price, regardless of brand loyalty; this is shown most dramatically in the shift away from product brands to retailer own labels in the supermarkets. Could this be because they are cheaper?

10
The Sales Force

There are few problems in running a company that cannot be improved by an increase in sales. A carefully chosen sales force can be a company's most dynamic generators of profits. But sales forces are expensive and you have to think carefully about what kind you need.

The main factor to be considered is do you want to deal directly with your end customers? If you do, and the product can bear the cost of direct distribution, then a sales force in the field will certainly give you much greater control of both your marketing and your profits. If the product cannot bear the cost, as is often the case in consumer goods, you have to choose between wholesaler and retailer distribution.

The wholesaler route reduces the costs of sales and administration because you need a much smaller sales team. However, your profits may suffer if you are forced to offer high discounts and you lose control in that you cannot build an exclusive relationship with customers. If you deal direct with retailers you have more control, but you need larger sales and administration teams and a bigger advertising budget.

Once you have decided that your sales force will be direct, retail, or wholesale-oriented, there are four further areas to consider:

1. Sales forecasting.
2. Management structure and control.
3. Territorial allocations.
4. Sales remuneration.

Sales forecast

The single most important task for sales management is to forecast the likely or possible volume of sales. Everything else depends on that.

There are many approaches to sales forecasting, both statistical and non-statistical, subjective and objective. Whichever your method, use commonsense to check the predictions. Do the salesmen think your forecast possible? Will the market bear such an increase in sales? Is your method relevant to the company? Furthermore, to subject a two-person company to the kind of econometric analysis normally reserved for Woolworth would be singularly non-productive.

Usually, the best method is a combination of both subjective and objective techniques. Valuable approaches are time series analysis, the examination of sales data over a period of time to look for seasonal patterns and general trends, and the use of simple trend projections (ie the growth in ice cream sales in January is 10 per cent each year, so it is estimated that for the following three years growth will be maintained at 10 per cent). These objective methods coupled with direct discussion with salesmen, direct competitors or in-house experts can produce meaningful results.

Two subjective methods of making forecasts are the Delphi method and Bayesian theory. The Delphi method uses a panel of perceived experts within the company which is asked specific questions about the sales environment and its likely growth. These answers are collated and represented to the group, which then has to provide a consensus answer to the original questions. Bayesian theory requires the sales management to make a number of sales projections and profit projections, and then allocate the probability of them being achieved. The multiplication of probability and a profitability factor indicate the best choice.

These methods are particularly valuable when you come to launching new products.

Once a company's forecast has been established, including, of course, sales management input, it must be 'owned' by the sales team. This is no easy task, as the lower the product targets the more secure the sales team will feel and the more assured of over-achieving. However, unless the product being sold is an infinite service – banking as against hotel rooms – production has to be geared to the expected sales volume. Over-achievement, can cause as many problems as under-achievement, with unfulfilled orders, upset customers and demoralised sales representatives. Sales ownership of individual targets is extremely important, and requires great managerial skill.

Managerial structure and control

Regardless of the size of the operation, effective organisation is a fundamental. The sales function can be structured in a number of ways, but there are basically three options:

1. *By product.* This leads to product managers with their own sales teams. This is the approach used, for instance, by the 3M Company and is commonly seen among the department stores where buyers exist separately for hardware, clothes, food, and so on.
2. *By customer.* As product diversification may be the basis for organisational structure, so might growth in different target customers. In life insurance, for instance, companies will have separate field forces to deal with insurance brokers and with the public direct.
3. *By location.* This is logical where the areas of sales coverage are too large for one sales function to administer. Saatchi and Saatchi have separate sales operations across Europe, the Middle East and North America to suit each continent's customers.

No method need be permanent. Xerox, the US copier company, had a product-oriented sales force, each sales representative specialising in one copier. Then, in 1985, it revamped the force, and now almost three-quarters of the team have been retrained to sell the whole range of copiers, and two dedicated customer teams have been created to sell specifically to dealers and government departments. The results have been impressive, with Xerox increasing its share of the copier market from 10 per cent in 1985 to 11.5 per cent in 1986, and its sales force being voted best in the business and systems section of *Sales and Marketing* magazine.

Span of management

Once a basis has been determined, the span of control, ie how many people one person will directly manage, needs to be determined. Usually, the numbers quoted are either seven, developed from psychological research, or 10, based on the Roman legionnaire model. What is certain is that too little attention paid to spans of management control will lead to unwieldy and frequently uncontrollable operations.

Controls

Many methods of monitoring sales force performance have been developed, generating a wealth of information (if only it all could be read, understood, communicated and then acted upon!). In designing a sales-reporting system, two major considerations should always be borne in mind:

1. Will the sales force devote too much time to completing them, causing lowering of morale and wasted sales time?
2. What information is gained must be actionable by the management.

The actual type of sales report will depend upon the company's markets. More detailed information would be required for one-off product manufacturing such as Lamborghini cars than for mass-marketed products such as chocolate bars.

The core of most sales reports are the *narrative* of individual calls and the *ratios* of overall calls. The narrative will cover different aspects of the individual transaction, including competitive brands used by the customer, the customer's preferred call times, discussions, and new business secured (or lost). The ratios will calculate the number of cold calls made, number of interviews arranged, number of sales made, and the amount of time spent travelling/waiting/attending to sales administration. This information enables the sales manager to evaluate his sales team and to see what kind of product his customers require, so giving the sales representative information he needs to improve his own time management.

Territories

The organisation of the field force into territories will obviously depend upon whether you are organising sales by product, customer or location.

No system of territories will be perfectly equitable. Some representatives will have further to travel, some have higher-spending customers, and some more seasonally interesting products. The basic objective is to provide sufficient and equitable workloads and sales potential for each sales representative. In order to evaluate the size of a territory, ratio analysis can be employed. This is done by estimating the number of calls required by each customer, then multiplying that by the number of customers available, and then dividing this figure by the number of calls a sales representative would be expected to make. For instance, if it is expected that a sales representative should make 200 calls a year, yet there are 300 customers each requiring on average four calls a year, then the territory is large enough for six representatives.

Remuneration

An effective sales remuneration package should:

1. Attract and keep the sales team motivated – the degree of commission will be key.
2. Be seen as fair.

It should also be simple to understand and economical to operate. The basic components of any sales package will include:

1. Guaranteed earnings.
2. Performance-related earnings.
3. Bonuses.
4. Expense allowances.
5. Perks – cars, pensions, medical insurance, and so on.

Each of the two extremes – straight salary and commission only – has its benefits. Straight salary gives security but not massive motivation, is often difficult to lower if markets decline, and usually means that regular cost-of-living adjustments are expected. Commission only, however, gives an income totally related to performance, which can be highly motivational but lead to short-term sales maximisation causing over-generous discounts, hard selling and misrepresentation. Commission only is obviously less secure than the straight salary method, and recipients would expect higher payments for comparable performance.

Sales team organisation and control are the cornerstones for all companies committed to personal selling. They are quite the most expensive method of satisfying customer needs for products and services; if they are not handled right they will fail, as will the company.

Part III: Implementation

Now that you have established the rough outlines of your marketing plan, the general objectives, budget and marketing mix (including the division between above- and below-the-line spending) comes the next step. This includes the process of implementation, selecting the agency, (or agencies), which will create your advertising and promotions, briefing them about strategy and advertising themes, and finally evaluating their work. (It is a good idea to keep your original plan flexible, and consult your agency before finalising it. As professionals, they are bound to have useful suggestions as to marketing mix.)

In many ways implementation is the really tricky part because you are so reliant on other people to realise your plans. You may think everything is running smoothly, but then your agency will present you with a campaign that is way-off course or a sales promotion that is very exciting but way over budget.

Care needs to be taken in choosing the right people to work with, and briefing them fully.

11
Creating a Promotion

Choosing an advertising agency

Some partnerships between clients and their advertising agencies seem to last for ever. Burmah Castrol has been with Dorlands for over 60, or even 70 years, (no-one seems to be quite sure which), though most partnerships are short-lived. A study in the USA by Ed Shields shows an average 'agency life' in the consumer field of three years, and seven years for industrial and business agencies.

The reasons partnerships break down are various, including factors such as changes of staff, invoice errors, problems in contacting people, and budget control problems. Or the company may have a new marketing director who wants to make his own personal mark.

The major factor that both causes a client to break with an old agency and seek a new one is creativity. Does the agency have the ability to put across your message in a way that is new and exciting? There are other matters which should also be on everyone's agency shopping checklists. They include:

- Experience – have they handled your kind of products before? If you are selling computers, do they know about them? But be careful because relevant advertising experience may not be a prerequisite even if relevant knowledge is. An agency that has not advertised computers before may be able to bring a totally fresh approach.
- Attitude – are they keen to work with you? Are you in danger of being an insignificant account in a big, impersonal agency? Should you opt for a small, thrusting agency, whose keenness

and caring may outweigh their lack of resources in certain departments?

- Understanding – how well do they understand your marketing as well as your technical problems?
- Other skills – do they have the additional skills which you may need, such as sales promotion, direct mail, public relations and conference organisation, or will you have to go elsewhere for these services?

Further questions worth asking are: Is the agency profitable? Is it winning business? What is the track record of senior management in previous jobs? While creativity is usually the first consideration, any of these other factors can outweigh it.

Styles of creativity

Creativity is a much used and misused word, covering a multitude of sins and virtues. If you are looking for a creative agency, it will pay to think about just what kind of creativity you want. Although this is potentially an endless subject, there are a few commonly recurring creative approaches to demonstrating a product, and different agencies tend to be better at it than others. The approaches include the use of:

- Presenters – often an expert, such as David Bellamy, or Magnus Pyke, to expound the product's virtues.
- Testimonials from a product user, such as a Pedigree Chum dogowner, saying how good it is.
- Dramatisations, showing people who use the product and benefit from it, including
  (a) 'The slice-of-life' - as in Procter and Gamble commercials, where a non-believer is presented with the product, uses it, and is converted.
  (b) Playlets – ranging from the documentary style in (a) to comedy playlets, as in most beer commercials.
- Brand symbols – a distinctive person or figure is used to symbolise the brand and its particular properties, like the

man from Del Monte or the Jolly Green Giant.

- Music – heightening the content of the commercial in one of three main ways:

  (a) Jingle – the slogan is set to music, as in Cadbury's 'finger of fudge' commercial, making it more memorable.

  (b) Musical – a big production number where people sing about the product; often, though, the commercial will swamp the product, which will get lost.

  (c) Theme music – memorable background music can considerably heighten the appeal of a commercial.

- Product demonstration – showing the product being used:

  (a) Before and after – the problem 'before' and the happy outcome 'after' the product is used.

  (b) Outperforming the competition – as in the Duracell commercials.

  (c) Torture tests – the watch continues to work 20,000 leagues under the sea.

- The pun – a lot of major campaigns, usually in press advertising have been based around puns, such as Perrier's 'Eau – H2Eau – Picasseau', and John Player's 'Black' posters.

It is true that these are just a few of the basic creative possibilities in presenting a product, but they will still help you to think about which kind of creative treatment, and therefore which agency you prefer. Some agencies are expert at the musical approach, some specialise in creating powerful brand symbols and identities, some are best at ingenious, but simple, hard-sell product demonstrations.

What they must also show is that all-important ability to have ideas, to twist the genres within which they work and so attract attention. Recent Budweiser commercials are an example. To some extent they fit within the musical genre – young men in a pub are inspired by Budweiser to sing songs to nubile girls. The idea, the twist that makes the commercial stand out, is the fact that the young men sing out of tune. (All the more courageous, therefore, and the more inspired by Budweiser.)

The problem in creating good advertising is to fuse creativity and hard sell, or, if you like, 'relevance'. The ideal is to have advertising that is creative, attention-grabbing *and* relevant to the product, with the excitement emerging directly from the product. Too often, creativity prevails at the expense of the sell, or vice versa.

Pitches

Once you have your checklist of questions, and have thought about what style of advertising you want, there are various ways of finding agencies.

Some people rely on their own knowledge of the agency scene. Others formally consult the *Advertising Agency Register* which will provide the name of appropriate agencies for a particular account. Others pick advertisements they like and find out who did them. Whichever method you follow, you are ultimately going to have to select by first making a shortlist of contenders.

At this point, a very common practice is to ask the agencies listed to pitch for the account. Almost all agencies will agree to do this, and usually free of charge. Only about 10 per cent of clients actually pay shortlisted agencies for pitching, though the number is growing. Few pay more than £5,000. The cost to agencies can vary from the £28,000 CDP claimed to spend on its American Soya Association pitch (which was lost) to £250,000 spent chasing £10 million plus accounts. The average cost of a pitch is about £30,000.

The advantage of pitches is that you do get various approaches to, and therefore various perspectives on your particular problems. And competition can stimulate some agencies to produce excellent work. David Horncastle, advertising and promotions manager of Honda, told *Campaign* that he found agencies' different interpretations of his brief fascinating. 'It would be nice to do it every year just to keep my ideas fresh about our product and our marketplace.'

Pitches are a form of test buying, providing you with an idea of the kind of work the agency produces. The disadvantage is that an agency may not be able to do its best work under these conditions, because it might require time to get to know you and your account. Also, appreciate that the people working on the pitch, (perhaps freelance writers) will not necessarily be the ones to work on the real advertisement.

The normal procedure for pitches is that you present agencies with a thorough advertising brief backed by comprehensive marketing data. Then you give them a fixed period within which to present a solution, preferably not less than four weeks, at the end of which you will receive full-scale presentations.

An alternative to pitches involves examining agencies in-depth, looking at the people who are going to handle your account, their strengths and weaknesses, and analysing the work they have done for other clients. Another approach involves using search consultants. They operate in the US and are already big business, their fees ranging from a modest £3,000 to as much as £200,000. Since selecting an agency can be so complex these fees are, in fact, thought to save money.

An interesting case of agency choice recently involved Fisons, the horticultural division of Fisons the chemical company. Its sales and marketing manager, John Gerry, decided in 1984 that he needed a new agency to launch a new range of products.

Gerry, who was familiar with the agency scene, plumped for the fashionable and highly successful Gold Greenlees Trott, because he felt they had the mixture of creative flair and hard, strategic thinking that he needed. GGT was asked to pitch, did so, and won the account.

Three years later Fisons had different needs. Now they wanted an agency with more technical ability, that could understand all the product attributes and that was also a full-scale service agency. This time Fisons took a more formal route. It sent a four-page specification of its requirement to the *Advertising Agency Register* which identified nine candidates, sending Fisons their company video tapes and literature.

Fisons now cut the list to four agencies, which were chosen to make a presentation, together with the incumbent agency, within four weeks. Each agency was visited and three were rejected. Two were asked to do further work and make another presentation. Boase Massimi Pollitt won the account.

Briefing

Having chosen an agency you have to brief it, providing full and precise details of your marketing plan: the budget; your proposed marketing mix; and, very important, how you want to position the product – the stategy the advertising must follow. In addition you must provide the necessary background information, which should include:

1. The product – everything about it from production processes to its composition, packaging, and after-sales service.
2. The competition.
3. The market – who buys the product, market share, and so on.
4. Previous advertising as well as competitors' advertising.

Your marketing plan does not have to be decided in advance, and you can consult the agency on almost every aspect of it. What is imperative is that you are clear about your thinking, and give the agency clear directives.

The positioning of your product is probably the main area where it is easy to be confused and confusing. Is the main advantage of your delivery service that it is:

(a) Economical.
(b) Reliable.
(c) Offers a choice of delivery periods.
(d) Delivers to any destination.
(e) The fastest.

Or is it a combination of these benefits? At some point you are going to have to take a decision and plump for one or two. But you can, at the briefing stage, list them all, and ask the agency to decide between them.

Evaluation

Normally the agency, once briefed, will go away, gestate creatively, and return with a detailed presentation. This will begin with a carefully argued reiteration of marketing background and advertising strategy, and proceed to creative execution and the 'idea'.

Then the agency team will turn to you expectantly for your verdict. A variety of not immediately relevant thoughts can pass through the marketing manager's mind, including: Could we ever afford to produce this? Will the sales force like it? Will my boss think I'm an idiot if I recommend this? Put these to one side. The first important question to ask: Is the advertising on strategy? Do not forget that it has to deliver the message. The naked woman or the severed head on the agency's proposed advertisement may be very striking, but have very little to do with the tractors you are selling. Also question whether the advertising is *clearly* on strategy, and if it is making one or two points concisely and understandably.

Equally, you have to ask: Is the advertising creative/exciting/attention-getting? It may be on strategy, but will people ever bother to read or consider the message? Will the target audience like it? As a 35-year-old marketing manager you may love it, but will it appeal to the 19-year-olds in Neasden who may be your core market?

You may also want to ask: Is this idea campaignable? Can it be carried right through your advertising material, including point of sale and exhibitions? Can it be developed? Is this commercial for Levis, that shows a man taking off his jeans in a launderette, a brilliant one-off, or does it 'have legs'? Could you show a whole series of people taking off their jeans in different situations? What does the agency think?

If the advertising successfully answers all these questions, it may be just what you are looking for.

Advertising research

If you can afford it, research your advertising before and after it runs. Many major agencies – Boase Massimi Pollitt being one of the great examples – rely heavily on research and will go through several stages of conceptualisation and testing before producing the final advertisement.

Qualitative research, using panels of potential customers, can give you some idea in advance of how people will respond to your campaign. Advertisements can be tested in any form, from names and concepts to roughs and storyboards, to printed advertisements and produced films. Research will show how well consumers remember the advertisements, how favourably they react to the strategy and execution, and any other responses you care to elicit. You may find that your supposedly sophisticated and fashionable advertising actually comes across as crude and laughable. Remember that people react very differently in front of their television, and do not always articulate their responses accurately, especially when confronted with something radically new. Nor, just because they like the advertisement, will they necessarily buy the product.

You can also research advertising while it is running. Dealer audit research is one invaluable tool. If you advertise in one town or area and not in another control district, this will tell you fairly accurately how advertising is contributing to sales, assuming the advertising does not involve special extras such as free offers. Also research, just after your product has appeared on television or in the press, can tell you how successfully and widely your advertising has communicated.

You can research long after the advertising has disappeared from view, which will help you work out whether it has truly registered your product in the public's mind, and has helped maintain or raise your sales.

Direct mail

Is it worth having a separate agency for direct mail? It all depends how good your main agency's direct-mail department or subsidiary is. A single agency handling all your requirements is much more convenient; an additional direct-mail agency may have much more enthusiasm and respect for direct mail and much wider experience.

The basic principles of selecting and briefing advertising and direct-mail agencies are much the same. The principles of evaluating direct mail are very different. What is successful in above-the-line advertising may not work in direct mail at all.

For example, good advertising is, as a rule, succinct. It makes its point simply and with as much impact as possible. A good letter is often *repetitive*. A classic DM dictum is: Say what you want to say, then say it, then say it again, then summarise it. The reasoning is, first, that a letter is more like a conversation than a formal piece of prose – and we need to have points repeated in conversation – and second, people often read letters in a disjointed way, so make sure that wherever they start reading, they cannot miss the point.

Also, where advertisements are often sparing with product *benefits*, good direct mail will give as many as possible. The advertisement may only be intended to draw attention, the letter has to get people to buy, and buy now, by providing a complete and convincing argument. (Letters which are intended to elicit enquiries can be much shorter.)

¡Box¿ :

This is called a Johnson Box. It is one of many direct mail techniques of drawing extra attention to information. Others are:

- Asterisks,
- Underlining,
- CAPITALS,
- Different typefaces.

Direct mail should still be *direct*. A good letter should get very quickly if not instantly to the product benefit. It should offer a *personal benefit*, directly related to the reader's needs.

In the USA, for example, two versions of the same basic letter were sent out to pension-plan administrators a few months after standards for investing pension-fund money were established under the Employee Retirement Income Security Act (ERISA). One started: 'Is the money in your company's pension plan being invested as well as it could be?' The other began: 'May I send you, free and without obligation, a brochure which tells about an *easy way to fulfil the ERISA requirements for your company's pension plan?*

The second, which to an outsider might seem less direct, actually pulled three times as many responses as the first, because the benefit was personal, related to the administrator rather than the pension plan.

Ideally, direct mail should contain an *incentive* to buy or act now – a discount if you buy within the month, a free gift if you buy within two weeks. Incidentally, nearly all direct mail contains a postscript or PS because it is almost always read, and is a useful area for making important points (sometimes the PS is produced in simulated handwriting and in another colour).

Another classic part of direct mail is the message on the envelope. An interesting message will get people to open your letter in the right frame of mind. A good example was the message on a *Psychology Today* envelope: 'Do you lock the bathroom door behind you, even when there's no one else in the house?' You have to read on. That was written by Bill Jayme, reputed to be the world's highest paid direct-mail copywriter, who receives up to £35,000 a package.

Reply cards can be very helpful in eliciting information. That used for the 3M Griddle Cleaning system is a good example. Here was a low-cost product designed for catering establishments. The problem was to identify potential customers, since little was known about the location of griddles.

So a list with a high proportion of fast-food outlets was mailed. A free sample of the product was offered, in return for which recipients had to complete a simple reply card, with tick box selections. The mailing elicited a 12.62 per cent response, and all returned cards were completed in full. An analysis revealed that griddles were much more common in non-fast-food outlets than had been thought, and the majority of griddles were being cleaned with stones or scrapers, which can damage the surface – a big selling point for 3M. Thus a simple reply card led to 3M's market being considerably widened.

The principles listed above are just a few of those which apply to direct-mail letters. Like any creative principles, they are there to be broken, although the direct-mail world rarely does break them. Some mainstream writers are appalled. Creative consultant, Martyn Hurst, for example, argued recently in *Campaign* that 'direct mail has a long way to go before it can take its place alongside imaginative, innovative and persuasive advertising'. But direct-mail writers will probably continue to follow the same basic principles for one simple reason – they work, they sell.

Where creativity has a much freer rein in direct mail is in the total mailing package. For example, one direct-mail agency had a very difficult problem. Research had shown that certain industrial equipment could only be bought if both the managing director and the engineering director okayed it. The problem was to get the two together. The ingenious mailing solution was to send one a mystery box, and the other the key. Human curiosity did the rest and, since the box contained important product information as well as a free gift, many valuable sales resulted.

Each item within a mailing package should be interesting in itself. At the same time, it should encourage the reader to proceed to the other items, and should reinforce the general message. A leaflet giving details of a free gift, for example, might include a reminder of the conditions of eligibility and the final date for responding.

The maximum number of enclosures in any package is usually taken to be seven. The cost for a pack of this size, for a mailing of approximately 100,000, would usually be in the region of £400 per thousand.

Case History No 10. Direct Mail: Murray Johnstone Olympiad

The Moorgate Group's launch campaign for the Murray Johnstone Olympiad Unit Trust is an excellent example of how powerful direct mail can be, and illustrates many important principles.

First (and also a general marketing principle) the product, an

international unit trust, was powerfully branded with the name
Olympiad conveying both 'international' and 'top performer'.
Large, money-off-the-page advertisements were placed in the
financial pages of the major dailies. At the same time, 1,000
financial intermediaries were supplied with direct-mail material
for their clients, including a personal letter to the broker.

The letter had a direct, distinctive opening, voicing the
consumer's natural scepticism with: 'Who are Murray Johnstone? And what can they do for you?' Several reasons were then
given for investing, including Murray Johnstone's investment
record, the advantages of both new and international trusts, and
the standing of Murray Johnstone in the international investment world. A valuable 1 to 2 per cent discount was offered for
early investment. And finally, the PS repeated the fact that the
bonus period would end soon. A lengthy and lavish brochure
was included which went into all the above advantages of an
international unit trust in still greater length.

The result? 600,000 clients were mailed and by the end of the offer period more than £29 million had been invested, a staggering figure for such launches. (A further £7 million was invested from the off-the-page advertisments and a separate mailing to 12,000 existing Murray Johnstone unit holders.)

12

Implementing Public Relations

Selecting a consultancy

You have three main options in selecting people to manage your PR. Your advertising agency may have its own department, you can go to an independent PR consultancy, or you can set up your own in-house PR.

Many large organisations, including government agencies, health authorities, educational bodies and fire services have their own in-house PR. The first advantage is that this provides a full-time service, which can be very important if you need a lot of PR. You PR officer can be on-hand up to 24–hours, and that can be useful in 'fire-fighting' situations, such as the salmonella discovery in Farley's factory. You may also save on the otherwise expensive fees you would pay an independent consultancy. Also, your in-house PR can get to know the company intimately, and have ready access to necessary information. On the other hand, they can be expensive if you do not have enough for them to do. Many UK companies, faced with the economic pressures of the 1980s, were forced to close or cut back their PR departments. And in-house PRs may not be sufficiently critical and independent-minded. Nor will they have the same breadth of experience as independents.

A PR department within your advertising agency has obvious advantages, it is convenient and well-placed to integrate and coordinate PR with advertising. On the other hand, the advertising can often inhibit and constrain public relations programmes.

An independent PR consultancy – there are more than 600 to choose from – is likely to provide the most independent advice.

It will probably bring wide experience in a variety of media, as well as extensive contacts to bear on your problem. It will also restrain the advertising agency from making exaggerated claims. PR firms are increasingly conscious of their liabilities. They know that erroneous information can have a range of consequences from consumer litigation to an action for defamation from a competitor to a tumbling share price. And, since they can be sued along with their clients, they are usually very careful.

If you want to find the names of consultancies, look at the *PRCA Public Relations Year Book,* but do not expect to set up a competitive pitch as with advertising agencies. Some consultancies may be prepared to present competitive propositions, though many will resent it and refuse. Since they bill by their time, they are much more aware of the expenses and possible losses involved in pitches.

Creating a PR programme

The first point to establish in creating a PR programme is what kind of image do you wish to project, and to whom? You have to define your *objectives* and *publics.* In order to reach those publics you must now select the *media* and *techniques.* And finally, your programme should include a *budget* and *methods of assessing results.*

First, you have to discover how people see you. An *image study* may be helpful. It will determine the current image of your company held by outsiders and compare it with the image held by your own managers. Alternatively, you or your PR people can conduct informal interviews. Think carefully about the image you are going to project because the obvious image and publics are not always the right ones.

Not so long ago, convenience foods were promoted as complex recipe ingredients in order to reassure housewives about the value of serving time-saving meals. Nowadays housewives are more sophisticated and are less inclined to have guilty consciences, so the projected image is more one of convenience.

Similarly, you may be able to achieve more by directing your PR at a different public. Cussons sales and marketing director, Colin Hession, recently took a very daring step for a FMCG manufacturer, in largely eschewing consumer PR and putting most effort into trade PR to enhance the trade's perceptions of Cussons. This had very positive business results.

Media releases

Press, television and radio releases are a very important element in the success of a PR programme, and close attention should be paid to them.

A good 70 per cent of press releases hit the dustbin. There would be nothing like that waste if only PR would follow certain basic principles.

1. *No product puffery.* The first, most sacred principle is that you cannot say 'Product X is wonderful', instead you have to offer hard news, something that will be of interest to a news station and the general public. You have to have an 'angle'. If you just say that a certain cereal manufacturer is offering five more flavours in a range, that is not news. If you can report that surveys show that children are now taking twice as long to select cereals because of the extra choice, that just might be news.

If you do send out releases with trivial content, the effect can be disastrous. Some companies send out an average of three press releases a week, and since no organisation is that interesting, the end result can often be that their releases are spiked automatically.

2. *Tailor the release.* A PR release has to be tailored to a given medium, being written so that chunks can be lifted straight out and reprinted in the paper. The video release has to be filmed so that it can be used within a given television programme, and the same applies to tapes for radio. This can only be achieved by examining target journals and programmes in detail.

Do not confine yourself to press releases because tapes can be very successful. It is true that some radio stations will not listen to them because they receive so many, and some even throw the tapes away and use the reels. But when IPC, which runs *Successful Slimming* magazine in conjunction with a national network of slimming clubs, sent out a series of 12 3- or 4-minute taped interviews with the managing director of the company to radio stations across the country, 15 stations accepted them.

3. *Send material to the right people.* Very often feature material sent into television and radio stations is passed on the news editor rather than the features producer, and therefore never gets used. A little research here can pay enormous dividends.

4. *Talk to the right people.* Pick up a phone and talk direct to editors and producers – they may be only too delighted to tell you what sort of stories they are looking for. Even better if you can actually meet them. Sounds obvious? Trevor Taylor worked on the radio programme *The Chip Shop* for 18 months – during which only two PR companies took the trouble to talk to him.

Case History No 11. Public Relations: Eagle Star's Rainbow Investments

The 1985 launch of Eagle Star's Rainbow Investments is a good example of a well-integrated and executed PR programme.

Eagle Star, a major insurance company, was not perceived as being an investment manager, despite massive experience in the field. So when it decided to launch a range of investments, including several unit trusts, there was an obvious need for PR to educate both press, public and even staff.

Key to the success of the programme was the innovative and highly user-friendly Rainbow concept, with all the investments being colour-coded according to the degree of risk involved. The programme involved:

1. Press lunches. The programme began five months before launch with a series of lunches inviting journalists to meet the chief executives of Eagle Star. It was correctly calculated that the very fact that a major financial firm such as Eagle Star was branching out would prove an enormous attraction.

2. A press conference was held nearer launch announcing the new Rainbow concept and attracting a record attendance by journalists.

3. Press releases were sent out giving details of the launch of the Rainbow Unit Trusts, Investment Bonds and Savings Plans. After the launch, further bulletins were sent out detailing the record sums of money attracted. (Even more helpful, Eagle Star was, a few months later, to win two awards for Best Small Unit Trust Group of the Year.)

4. A specially recorded 3-minute interview with marketing director John Douglas was distributed to radio stations across the country, receiving several plays.

5. Financial intermediaries were invited to roadshows held around the country, introducing the Rainbow range in dramatic style, and featuring ex-newscaster Angela Rippon. The local press were also invited.

6. A special Rainbow Trail for Cub Scouts was sponsored.

7. Keen-eyed Eagle Star staff noticed that a Mrs Rainbow had invested in the new range. Cue for her well-published invitation to lunch.

8. The Rainbow launch was featured prominently in Eagle Star's in-house journal. Another step taken, and an innovative one, was to send branch offices cuttings of press coverage following launch. Staff were both involved and enthused.

The whole programme was well thought through, and the immediate result was enormous press coverage. Some 106 articles were written on the Rainbow range in the major dailies alone, with 46 articles in local papers. Coverage was very favourable, strongly replaying the Rainbow concept with headlines such as 'The Eagle Star's Colours Fly Over the Rainbow' and 'Eagle Star's Dash of Colour'. John Douglas commented: 'We would never have achieved this exposure without a sound PR programme.'

Financially, the launch was an immense success. Within six months some £37 million was invested in the Rainbow Bond and the Rainbow Unit Trusts. Eagle Star had come from nowhere to be a major *investment* force in the sector.

Assessing PR

Assessing results should be an essential part of any PR programme, although many clients are tempted to omit and save on costs.

There are various methods. The most immediate is to assess media coverage. First you tot up the total audience reached. If your story appears in three different papers with estimated readerships of two million, six million and one million, you can say that nine million people had the opportunity of reading it. Then you have to calculate the number of times that audience gets to take in your message – the 'OTS' rating. The same principles apply to coverage on television or in any other medium.

Another method involves doing an attitude study or taking an opinion poll pre- and post-PR. If awareness of your company has risen significantly, you can count your campaign a relative success. If awareness has dipped, you must be doing something very wrong!

Finally, you can talk directly and informally to members of your public. That is what Burson Marsteller did with architects in the case of Styrofoam covered earlier in this book.

13
Creating Sales Promotion and Merchandising

Using a sales promotion consultancy

If you ask most companies what they require of a specialist promotions consultancy (or indeed ask the consultancy itself), the chances are the answer will be creativity. In fact, while no client is averse to using a good new idea, the most usual reason for a consultancy is to save time (according to research findings gleaned from a recent MAPS [Marketing, Advertising and Promotions] exhibition).

If your budget is less than £6,000, you will not find many takers for your account anyway. £15,000 is a fairly average budget; £50,000 quite high; very few companies would expect to spend over £200,000 per annum on a product. Certainly, you should have a very clear idea of your objectives long before you execute them: failure to do so is likely to result in a runaway budget. As with exhibitions and conferences, it is common to plan events a year or so ahead and allocate an annual budget.

Again, it cannot be emphasised enough how important the role of coordination is to the successful outcome of a sales promotion. Most companies which retain the services of consultancies demand a variety of services from them including: design/artwork; print buying; competitions; point of sale expertise; trade incentives; direct mail; video; sponsorship; staff incentives; and on-pack offers, to name but a few.

But it should not be imagined that hiring a consultancy is going to solve all your organising and planning problems. Activities have to be coordinated interdepartmentally within the company. Promotions are unlikely to succeed without the help of the sales and production departments. And it is probably desirable to keep the company advertising agency and PR consultancy posted on events.

Some sales promotion agencies offer specialised auxiliary field forces as part of their package deal, which is usually a requirement with merchandising activities. If not, you may find yourself having to organise specialised training for the task within your own company's sales force. However, most consultancies should be able to sort out satisfactory arrangements with outside suppliers such as printers, manufacturers of merchandise for premium offers, distributors of coupons, and indeed retailers.

Probably the best place to start looking for a suitable consultancy is the *Institute of Sales Promotion Consultancy Register* (telephone 08956-74281). The essential point is to obtain a client list. As with advertising agencies it is desirable to find out the quality of existing clients and whether the consultancy has previous experience in your product area. One important difference, however, is that sales promotion consultancies generally manage to avoid the account conflict problems which preclude advertising agencies from handling more than one major client in a particular product area at a time. The reason is that promotion agencies are usually retained for particular projects rather than for long-term strategic purposes, as happens with agencies. So do not be unduly concerned if you find a consultancy which seems to have the right credentials, but also retains one of your rivals as a client.

Apart from enquiring about the range of marketing services on offer, you should also gain some idea of the quality of the consultancy by examining the number of ISP awards it has to its credit. Advertising agencies will sometimes provide you with leads but beware – many have their own sales promotion consultancy section. What may be in their interests is not necessarily in yours. You should carefully weigh up the quality of service against the benefits of agency/consultancy synergy (and possibly reduced costs) before committing yourself.

Organising exhibitions, conferences and seminars

There is no sure-fire means of setting out on paper how to organise conferences, exhibitions and seminars. Each has unique requirements, and fulfilling them successfully is something which demands both experience and luck. However, it is possible to impart a few short-cuts, and to demonstrate how apparently absurd yet easily made mistakes may be avoided.

Let us take conferences and meetings first. The first choice facing a company is whether to organise the event itself or farm it out to an expert. Whatever happens, responsibility for planning, scheduling and conducting the event must finally rest with one person, otherwise there will be tears. Increasingly, these events are being organised by what are called professional meeting managers, of whom there are over 12,000 in the USA alone. The best place to start looking for advice is in the specialist magazines such as *Conferences and Exhibitions International*, which offers a mine of information including facts and figures on venues, and a critical analysis of their suitability.

The recognised bible for conference venues is the *Conference Blue Book*, which is produced annually by Spectrum Communications. Together with the *Green Book*, a companion volume of specialist venues featuring sports and leisure facilities, it offers conference organisers an overall view of what is available in the UK.

Most leading towns and cities in the UK publish their own books and leaflets offering detailed local information. Many of the hotel groups also have their own conference packs, detailing what is available and how much it costs. Some, such as THF and Crest, will now offer you specialist conference coordinating services which promise to solve any permutation of requirements ranging from hauling a car into a hotel bedroom to setting up a complex video conferencing system.

Whatever the purpose of your conference or meeting, you should choose its location with great care. Here are a few hints. It is tempting to choose a spectacular and probably inexpensive setting far from your base. Resist such temptation: distance and inaccessibility, particularly in winter, are death to a meeting.

Carefully calculate how many of those invited are likely to turn up (as opposed to how many invitations were sent out). It may seem obvious that capacious facilities would solve this problem at a stroke. In fact, if anything, it is better to create the impression of a packed environment, while avoiding some of the inconvenience that may accompany overcrowding (the illusion of a capacity meeting may be created by deft use of manoeuvrable partitioning). The more compact the crowd, the more chance a speaker has of maintaining audience interest in his subject matter.

Examine the shape of the room and check that the speaker is visible from every corner, and that none of the seats are hidden behind massive pillars. Other important matters to consider, if the attention of the audience is not to wander, are air conditioning, light, temperature, and the absence of outside noise.

Proper ventilation, temperature control and probably air conditioning can make all the difference between a rapt audience and one which is literally half-asleep. Also smoking can be a major irritant. But obtrusive noise is the real 'killer', a problem which is easily overlooked. Check out the sound-proofing, ensure the hotel kitchens are not in shouting distance and that something resembling the Rio Carnival is not about to take place in an adjoining area.

Even blue chip companies and their conference organisers can commit silly mistakes through lack of commonsense, the enemy of a successful event. A major motor manufacturer poised to launch a new car could find no suitable venue for three consecutive weeks. The production company it had retained finally decided to solve the problem by erecting a huge hi-tech marquee and to place the entire show in that.

A perfectly flat floor was required, and earth was excavated by a couple of inches to make the ground absolutely level. Then a pit was dug, and the car place in it, waiting to be unleashed on a unsuspecting audience.

All this preparation had taken place during a dry summer week. The very day the show opened, it poured with rain.

Result: the marquee flooded and rainwater filled the carefully excavated pit. Easy to overlook, though, was it not?

Placement agencies

The fact that there is a general shortage of good conference centres in the UK, and that the few that exist tend to be booked up in the short-term makes a fairly compelling argument for using a conference placement agency, of which there are over a dozen in the UK. Some, such as the London Convention Bureau (LCB) and Association of Conference Executives (ACE International), act in an advisory capacity, providing lists of venues and sometimes the opinions of previous users of them. Others, such as Expotel, provide a full service including costing and organisation. (Interestingly, placement agencies derive their income from commission charged not to the client, but to the venue owner eventually selected.)

Recent published statistics show that exhibitions are becoming a major rival to the media. One reason for the amount being spent is undoubtedly the fact that marketing men find them an increasingly attractive alternative to the rising costs of the press, television, and so on. But this should not deceive. The swelling expenditure on exhibitions is also a product of the staggering increase in space rental and stand construction (which is 700 to 800 per cent more than it was 15 years ago).

The moral is look very carefully at the way you exhibit your products to make sure you are getting value for money. One of the most significant features of the recent International Business Show at Birmingham's National Exhibition Centre was the number of empty spaces caused by the non-appearance of many traditional exhibitors.

Blanket coverage and corporate flag waving are giving way to speciality exhibitions, smaller, usually with a regionally-based location, and often private (which includes launches held in hotels, in-store exhibitions and shopping precinct displays). Certain inferences about the preparation for exhibitions may be drawn from this trend. One is that research and planning are becoming more important than ever before.

Planning should start months ahead, even up to a year. Do not be tempted to move in at the last moment. The shoddiness of last-minute preparation almost always manages to communicate itself to visitors and leaves an impression of lack of professionalism.

You can find out a lot about the calendar for forthcoming exhibitions and trade fairs by consulting the exhibition bulletin, *British Rate and Data* (generally known as *BRAD*), and from enquiries to trade associations, the Department of Trade and Industry, and local chambers of commerce. The next step is to gain quotations from exhibition organisers for their rates per square foot, and to obtain a layout of the proposed exhibition.

As with conferences, quite a lot is down to the application of commonsense, so ensure the exhibition venue is appropriate for your kind of product and that you have not rented some obscure nook or cranny where no-one will notice you. When booking space, it is also advisable to relate the timing to an advertising schedule. Local advertising helps to alert people in the vicinity to the fact there is something worth seeing. National advertising can form an especially useful complement when a new product is being launched.

A crucial consideration is the design of your stand: design is often where the battle is won or lost and requires the services of a professional. Get quotations from several companies. You will want to repeat the process with other suppliers such as photographers, printers, models, maybe even an auxiliary field force, to get an early idea of costings. Often these matters can be dealt with through a single agency which will offer a package price.

In the bigger purpose-built exhibition venues, you may want to use a preexisting 'shell' (which can be very expensive). In that case you will quickly need to contact the exhibition promoter. But given the increasing trend towards private exhibitions, and rising costs, lightweight modular one-piece display systems are now much more in vogue. Most of these rely on the panel-and-pole principle. Panels of various sizes are connected to vertical poles to form virtually every size or shape of display stand imaginable. They can be clipped together at almost any angle, allowing all sorts of permutations of design. The panels themselves are usually faced with loop-nylon plastic, to which Velcro can be attached. So, once set up, it is easy to attach the required graphics such as photographs, poster material and polystyrene letters.

Another extremely popular development has been the folding one-piece display system. The normal set-up is two tiers of four panels, each approximately three-feet high and about two-feet wide. Easily erectable, they will also fold down into a carrier bag.

Probably the best way of underlining the importance of professional design skills in laying out an exhibition stand is to cite an example. Brake Brothers (Frozen Foods) Ltd regards exhibitions as a very important vehicle for signing up new business, gaining extra business from existing customers, and increasing the number of prospects.

The problem for the company designing its stands at Hotelympia – Davies Virgo and Associates – was how to give effective visibility to over 600 product lines without cluttering the stand. It was overcome by using a series of large-scale photographs displaying a wide range of Brake Bros products which were mounted along the rear wall of the exhibition area, above 10 large refrigerators containing the products.

The right-hand side of the 76 square metre display area was designated a dining area where salesmen could encourage customers to sample food and sign up orders. There was also a large kitchen/store area necessitated by the preparation of food for sampling: a refrigerated glass showcase completed the stand.

The other matters you will need to keep a close eye on are liaison with the exhibition organiser's press officer in order to take full advantage of any pre-event publicity. Also ensure that he is kept abreast of any new developments by issuing properly prepared releases (retain the press packs for your own display area). And finally, ensure that any of your staff officiating at the exhibition have been booked into nearby hotel accommodation at the right time.

14
Creating a Sales Force

Your marketing plan may be a positive masterpiece, but the odds are you will still need a sales team to implement it. And if you cannot recruit the right salespeople your whole marketing strategy may have to go by the board.

Recruitment

Before you undertake any recruitment activity you have to establish clearly what the company requires of sales representatives. The following questions must be answered:

1. What is the task of the sales representative?
2. What degree of specialised knowledge is required?
3. What remuneration package will be made available?
4. How will the representative be introduced to the company?
5. What training will be given?
6. How many sales representatives will be required?

Recruitment advertising is the usual way of announcing sales vacancies. Depending upon the number required, and the size of the company, a specialised agency can be engaged to present suitable candidates from within its files, or the work can be undertaken by the company itself.

Currently, the most utilised medium is press advertising, either trade magazines or national/regional newspapers. Local radio, though, is becoming more and more popular. The economics here vary enormously. Recruitment agencies work on retainers or on payment for successful recruitment; their fees are related to the perceived difficulty of the task. However, it may be possible to produce within the company advertising copy that is just as effective and much cheaper.

The following breakdown gives some idea of the costs involved:

Medium	Cost £	Size
National newspaper (display)	3,000	20 cm × 3 column
National newspaper (classified)	8	Per column line
Regional newspaper (display)	500	20 cm × 3 column
Regional newspaper (classified)	4	Per column line
Trade magazine	500	Half page
Local radio*	2,400	12 × 30-second spots

* Particularly useful for mass introductory sessions

Production costs vary, but for a press advertisement expect to pay around £100 plus VAT, and for a local radio commercial around £150 plus VAT. The average cost of a recruitment agency is 15 per cent of the first-year's salary.

What you put in an advertisement depends on how well-known your company is, whether it wants to be known, who it wants to attract and where the advertisement is placed. Three things should always be included: what is on offer; which sales people should apply; and how to make contact.

Other methods of recruitment include word-of-mouth, referrals from existing staff, recruitment from non-sales staff, and the attraction of 'star' performers in rival firms.

Selection process

Individual or panel interviewing will be necessary. If a large number of appointments are going to be made, then seminar discussions can be both economical and effective. Here, groups of people are invited to hear what the company has to offer and, for those who are interested, a further personal interview can be arranged. Where resources allow, personal interviews can take place at the initial stage. Screening of applicants can be achieved by requesting a *curriculum vitae* or by the completion of a suitably-designed application form.

The whole objective of the interview procedure is to match the person with the job. Unfortunately, there are no 'right' characteristics. American research has shown that empathy and ego drive – that strong, personal need to make the sale – are likely base traits, but whether the candidate is introvert or extravert seemingly makes little difference. A number of psychometric tests are available which can help to describe the applicant and screen out those who are at the extremes, but a good judgement, based upon experience aided by these tests, seems to be the surest way to succeed.

Training

Once the sales person or persons have joined the company, some training should be given. Assuming that the candidate already has a strong understanding of, and can exhibit his ability in salesmanship, the prime initial function of training is to provide the sales people with a sound understanding of the company, its products and its customers. The type and format of the training will depend upon the degree of customer awareness and hence the level of product knowledge necessary.

In industrial goods, a good understanding of the whole market is essential to ensure product acceptance. Training can be organised centrally, or can be decentralised; it can be conducted by the company's own staff or by external consultants. It can be of long duration or short. But whatever format is chosen the training programme must be continuous and motivate people to work. Even where a specific need does not require immediate attention, an external course or a trip to central office can give a salesman the vital extra edge to his work. External courses are not cheap. For non-residential courses, expect to pay between £75 and £100 a day, for residential courses anything up to £1,000 a week.

In 1986, the *American Publication Sales and Marketing Magazine* carried out its annual review of American sales forces. Without exception, all the top ranking companies scored high on their staff training. This was particularly true of Xerox, Black and Decker and IBM.

Motivation

This much-used, and perhaps over-used word is often described as the key to a successful sales team. If your team is motivated, the occasional office mistake will not matter, but if the team is demoralised any excuse will be found to blame others for lack of sales. This is where the role of the sales manager is most demanding. He is the interface between the salesperson and his company. He has to explain the inexplicable, he has to cope with his own and his team's disappointments, and he shares and enjoys the successes.

In most organisations, motivational campaigns are set up centrally, seeking to create peer status for the winner and directing the whole sales team towards the company's goals. However, where a large sales team exists, group or regional campaigns and competitions can be encouraged, provided they are developed to achieve specific goals and do not restrict the overall objective of the company.

Sales people are motivated by many different things, and it is a great mistake to believe that the sole motivation of a salesman is financial reward. It may be a prestigious car, peer group recognition or a new title. It is the organisation's role to identify what will encourage that extra effort and evaluate the cost of (a) not providing it, (b) increased business and (c) the reduction in morale of other members of the sales team. If a positive answer is arrived at, the organisation should activate the change.

Most motivational campaigns are based on the theory of the hierarchy of needs: that a person first needs to secure his lifestyle, then needs status and, finally, seeks self-fulfilment. Designing motivational programmes has become a specialist art, and a number of agencies now offer consultancy advice.

The most basic of needs is the desire to be needed: a role only achievable on a one-to-one basis. Here the manager is all-important, requiring the ability to coach, empathise and encourage. Opportunities for motivating in this way occur regularly at sales meetings and personal focal points, such as the annual appraisal. Sales meetings should be instructive, dynamic and motivational in themselves. Objective analysis of the group's achievements against targets can be communicated, successes applauded, failures analysed, peer-group recognition given and team spirit built to maintain the salesman in his usually isolated role. These meetings also provide an opportunity to give a wider company view.

The performance appraisal, correctly handled, can give a massive injection of enthusiasm and drive, even to the poor performer. Handled wrongly, it can ruin a relationship and career. The appraisal meeting is a time to set targets, goals and objectives for the following review period. Of course, depending on the circumstances, they can be as frequent as the sales situation requires. Perhaps the best example of this type of management involves treating employees as people not personnel.

Coca-Cola is a perfect example of where the appointment at senior level of a new head of sales turned a company suffering from the failure of New Coke, revitalised its sale initiatives, regained its number one position from Pepsi in the cola market, and captured 39 per cent of the US soft drink market. The difference was the man. He was regarded by the sales team as understanding their role, having been a successful salesman himself and being regarded as a good manager.

If you have any doubts about the value of a sales team, ask IBM. Despite falling market share the IBM sales team is consistently ranked first in the computer market. It is generally agreed that the team's quality kept IBM's lower revenues in 1986 from being even worse than they were. IBM are showing their confidence in their salesmen by creating 24 new sales offices, increasing the sales team by 20 per cent, and repositioning from a geographical to an industry orientation. The moral is do not automatically cut your sales team when the market changes, adapt it, and even expand it.

15
Conclusion

It used to be said that Britain was way behind America in its understanding of the importance of marketing. In the past few years that situation has been changing rapidly. More and more British companies are waking up to the fact that business and industry must be marketing-led – and one proof is that marketing people are increasingly in demand.

There are three main principles in being market-led – principles we have seen time and again in this book. The first is that a company must concentrate, as far as it is able, on satisfying the consumer's needs. That sounds obvious in theory, but it is not in practice because the natural human urge is to concentrate on one's own needs as a producer, to tell people what a wonderful product this is, what a wonderful piece of engineering, how many man-hours it took to produce, how many tests it has passed, and how many credentials the company has. But most consumers could not care less. They want to know what is in it for them. Marketing people have to learn to see the product through the customer's eyes, and communicate clearly how the product can help them. To simplify somewhat, they have to learn to see a car as a form of transport first, and only second as a car or piece of machinery.

The next major principle is that marketing must be planned. Again it sounds obvious, but in practice people tend to rush in, and think and philosophise later. A marketing manager must, like any good manager, form a plan of what his sales objectives are and how he is going to achieve them through a marketing mix. For each part of that mix, for advertising, public relations, sales promotion, he must set further, specific objectives. Then, as in any good management plan, there must be a means of assessing whether targets are being reached, and contingency arrangements which allow for changes of plan.

Third, marketing managers must realise that every part of their marketing effort – from overt advertising, to packaging and salesmen and visiting cards – is, whether they like it or not, a communication about the product. Marketing must be carefully thought out and coordinated in all its aspects. No part is automatically superior or inferior to any other. A direct-mail campaign or a small advertisement in a local newspaper may be far more effective in certain cases than a major television campaign. Alternatively, a television campaign may in certain cases prove to be not only more effective but cheaper than less prestigious media.

All these principles, properly followed, can mean a great deal of initial extra effort for marketing managers. Analysing carefully exactly what you have to offer consumers, and what you are going to tell them, can be a very time-consuming business. But, once you have precise analyses and objectives, you do not have to keep redefining yourself each time a new problem arises. In the end, these principles make life so much simpler.

Addresses

Advertising and Media

Advertising Association
15 Wilton Road
London SW1V 1NS
01–828 2771

Advertising Film & Videotape Producers Association
48 Carnaby Street
London W1V 1PF
01–434 1482

Creative Services Association
24 Nutford Place
London W1H 57N
01–723 3484

History of Advertising Trust
Abford House
15 Wilton Road
London SW1V 1LT
01–828 4831/2

Incorporated Advertising Management Association
c/o Advertising Association (see above)

Incorporated Society of British Advertisers
44 Hertford Street
London W17 8AE
01–499 7502

Institute of Practitioners in Advertising
44 Belgrave Square
London SW1X 8QS
01–235 7020

International Media Buyers' Association
c/o Wasey, Campbell, Ewald Ltd
30 Eastbourne Terrace
London W2 6LD
01–262 3424

London Advertisement Managers' Association Ltd
147 Fleet Street
London EC4A 2HN
01–353 5555/8

Overseas Press & Media Association Ltd
122 Shaftesbury Avenue
London W1V 8HA
01–734 3052

Publicity Club of London
12 Duchy Road
Hadley Wood
Barnet EN4 0HX
01–449 3472

Radio Marketing Bureau
Regina House
259–269 Old Marylebone Road
London NW1 5RA
01–258 3705

Direct Marketing

Association of Mail Order Publishers Ltd
1 New Burlington Street
London W1X 1FD
01–437 0706

Association of Shared Mailing Organisers
17 Staveley Way
Brixworth
Northants
0604-881889

British Direct Marketing Association
1 New Oxford Street
London WC1A 1NQ
01–242 2254

British List Brokers Association Ltd
c/o List Management Services Ltd
122 Shaftesbury Avenue
London W1V 7DS
01–724 0560

Direct Mail Producers Association
34 Grand Avenue
London N10 3BP
01–883 7229

Marketing

Association of Export & Marketing Executives
PO Box 70
London E13 8BQ
01–552 6325

Association of Market Survey Organisations Ltd
Research Centre
Westgate
London W5 1EL
01–997 5555

Institute of Marketing
Moor Hall
Cookham SL6 9QH
06285-24922

Market Research Society
175 Oxford Street
London W1R 1TA
01–439 2585

Marketing & Promotion Association
133 Regency Street
London SW1P 4AG
01–630 9393

Marketing Society Ltd
35 South Park Road
London SW19 8RR
01–543 5191

Incentive Marketing

British Promotional Merchandise Association
21–25 Lower Stone Street
Maidstone ME15 6YT
0622-671081

Industrial Marketing

Industrial Marketing Research Association
11 Bird Street
Lichfield WS13 6PW
05432-23448

Sales Management

Institute of Sales & Marketing Management
31 Upper George Street
Luton LU1 2RD
0582-411130

Institute of Sales Promotion
13–15 Swakeleys Road
Ickenham UB10 8DF
08956-74281/2

Institute of Sales Technology & Management Ltd
91 Buckingham Palace Road
London SW1W 0RP

Managing & Marketing Sales Association
PO Box 6
Knutsford
Cheshire
060684 4511

Organisation of Professional Sales Agents
Trafalgar House
Grenville Place
Mill Hill
London NW7 3SA
01–959 3611

Society of Sales Management Administrators Ltd
19 Half Moon Lane
Herne Hill
London SE24 9JU
01–274 9533

Direct Selling Association Ltd
44 Russell Square
London WC1B 4JP
01–580 8433

Public Relations

Association of Women in Public Relations
c/o Argos Distributors
112 Station Road
Edgware HA8 7AQ
01–951 1363

Institute of Public Relations
Gate House
St John's Square
London EC1M 4DH
01–253 5151

Public Relations Consultants Associations
10 Belgrave Square
London SW1X 8PH
01–245 6444

Society of County & Regional Public Relations Officers
County Offices
Matlock DE4 3AG
0629-3411

Society of District Council PROs
Borough of Eastleigh Civic Offices
Leigh Road
Eastleigh SO5 47R
0703-614646

Marketing Publications

Market Research Society Year Book (01–235 4709)
Organisations providing market research services in Great
Britain
Market Research Society

International Director of Market Research Organisations (01–235
4709)
International market research organisations
Market Research Society

The Marketing Year Book (06285-24922)
Specialist organisations providing a variety of marketing ser-
vices: promotion, advertising, packaging, exhibitions, etc
Institute of Marketing

Guide to Official Statistics (01–928 1321)
Covers all official and significant non-official sources of statistics
HMSO

The Creative Handbook (0342-26972)

British Rate and Data (BRAD) (01–434 2233)
National guide to media selection
Maclean Hunter Ltd

PNA Media Link (01–377 2521)
Media contacts and listings
PNA Service Ltd

The Blue Book of British Broadcasting (01–405 7151)
Broadcasting, radio, television, cable and satellite Who's Who
Telex Monitors Ltd

Editors (01–251 9000)
Six volumes of UK media directories
London Information News Distribution Agency Ltd

Marketing Journals

Campaign
01–402 5266
Data Base Marketing
05806-5161
Direct Marketing World
05806-5161
Direct Response Magazine
0992-501177
European Journal of Marketing
0274-499821
Finance Direct
05806-5161

Food Marketing
0274-499821
IMRA (Industrial Marketing Research Association) News
0543-263448
Incentive Today – The Sales Promotion Magazine
0273-206722
Industrial Marketing Digest
0306-880822
Industrial Marketing and Purchasing
0274-499821
Marketing
01–402 1231
Marketing Week
01–439 9381
Media Week
01–353 9804
Money Marketing
01–439 4222
PR Week
01–353 9801
Promotion Marketing
0322-77788
Promotions and Incentives
01–688 7788
Sales and Marketing Management
0582-456767
What's New in Marketing
01–855 7777

Index

169